The People's History

North Shields
Plodgin' Through The Clarts

by

Norman Christenson

The house on the right used to be number 58 where the Christenson's lived through most of the 1930s and '40s. It was then a two up and two down and we lived in the lower left flat. The right hand tree is new but the one on the left looks awfully like the original where Silkey's ghost used to hang out.

First published in 1999 by

The People's History Ltd
Suite 1
Byron House
Seaham Grange Business Park
Seaham
Co. Durham
SR7 0PY

ISBN 1 902527 61 5

Contents

Appleby stairs, off Clive Street in the 1930s.

Introduction

Memory's a funny thing isn't it? I once knew a bloke who had this amazing ability to memorise numbers. One of his party tricks was to get four or five people to give him a banknote which he'd examine and hand back. Half an hour later he'd recite each note number in full with the name of whoever it belonged to. Similarly when I was what my wife laughingly refers to as 'a proper man' (ie at work) I'd live in awe of colleagues who could reel off masses of statistics without ever referring to charts or tables, whereas I'd write them down one minute and promptly forget them the next. Sometimes I even have trouble remembering my own car registration although to be fair I've only had it twelve years and it's not the sort of thing you read every day.

But memories don't have to be perfect records that you would willingly swear to in a court of law. Fond ones can be stored and nurtured and tinted to the desired rose coloured hue while less pleasant ones can be conveniently stashed away only to be unearthed during rare fits of depression. Ask any historian for an accurate picture of North Shields in the 1930s and they'd conjure up a depressing scenario of a grimy industrial township lashed by the freezing winds that howled in from the North Sea and cursed with massive unemployment, grinding poverty and back-breaking labour for those 'lucky' enough to have a job. But ask someone (like myself) who just happened to be born there around about that time and you'd get a completely different answer.

There isn't any logical reason why anyone with even a grain of sense would claim to be pleased to have been born in such a place and at such a time. Smack in the middle of the great depression, a short fourteen years after the end of one war and only seven years away from the start of an equally appalling conflict. Although we couldn't know it at the time, we'd be destined to see changes more dramatic and astounding than any that had taken place in many lifetimes before us. And, even better, we were born into a world that was still very much a place of innocence and wonder. Large tracts of it had still to be discovered or explored and so many of the things we take so much for granted today were still only being hinted at in Saturday afternoon *Flash Gordon* serials. Most of the kids we grew up with had never ridden in a motor car, spoken on a telephone or even seen an aeroplane let alone flown in one. Escalators, automatic doors, ball point pens, aerosol cans, frozen foods, computers, calculators, cling wrap, tea bags, shopping trolleys, and a host of other things we take so much for granted today were all still waiting to be invented. As indeed were comfortable shoes, socks that didn't fall around your ankles, collars that didn't cut your throat, and zippers that replaced the rows of fly buttons that men fumbled and swore at and worried about for their entire adult life.

Not only was our world a far simpler and less sophisticated place, it was also a much smaller one. It's more than likely that if you drew a circle with a radius of five miles from where we lived that most of us wouldn't have been outside it more than a handful of times by the time we reached adulthood. Milk, bread, coal and our other daily requirements were delivered by stout horses and creaking carts so that the roads were a safe and much used playground for us kids who could wander far and wide in this traffic-free environment. And wander we did as our little white legs took us up Johnny Pie Hill, around Billy Mill, across the Red Burn, up and down the Tiger Stairs and a host of other similarly exotic spots where, if my memory is correct, the sun always shone from a clear blue sky. We were doubly blessed to live on the side of a river with its perpetual comings and goings, its quays and docks and shipyards and rocks and jetties and landings where you could always while away an hour or two watching ships, catching crabs, throwing stones or hanging around till your clothes dried so you could go home without having to be told 'for the thousandth time' to keep away from that water. There was also a great selection of magnificent beaches and rolling headlands which, sadly, for most of our childhood, we could only admire through a tangle of barbed wire as we awaited the invasion of the dreaded Hun.

And all of that brings us back to memories. Memories of an ordinary place and the people who would invariably have described themselves as just ordinary people. Most of them never became famous or held high office, unless you count acting unpaid lance corporal as high office. They survived incredible hardships and yet were almost universally considerate, generous and scrupulously honest in their dealings with one another. They also shared a hard-edged sense of humour that was part and parcel of their breed and a sing song guttural dialect that is magnificent if you're born to it and totally incomprehensible if you aren't. The area they inhabit will never rate highly on the international tourist circuit but it has (or had) a bleak and rough charm to match that of its natives. Absence is reputed to make the heart grow fonder and the fact that my wife and I left the old town to make our Australian fortunes way back in 1957 may, in part, account for some slight tendency to exaggerate. Certainly we find changes each time we return to the bosoms of our respective families, but none of this affects my memories which are guaranteed to be an absolutely accurate and unbiased view of life in 'Shields' during the 1930s, '40s and '50s. If they do happen to be wrong in any particular detail, please don't let me know as I still have to live with them.

Norman Christenson

SECTION ONE

CANNY OLD SHIELDS OUR BETTER HALF

Northumberland Park.

The Gibraltar Rock.

The town of North Shields is part of the County Borough of Tynemouth which in turn is part of England's northernmost county, Northumberland or Northumbria as it used to be when it was an ancient kingdom. Some latter day politicians decreed that it now sits in an area called Tyne and Wear but this can be dismissed as a temporary aberration. The Borough splits into two quite distinct halves. Tynemouth, as its name implies, sits at the entrance to that great coaly river and is the posh half of the Borough. It has its own posh golf club, its own posh tree lined streets where posh business people polish posh cars in front of posh bungalows. We never knew anybody who lived at Tynemouth although Wor Ma did char for a really nice woman in Dean Road. Nearer the coast, the bungalows gave way to the older part of the Borough where white haired women in colourful 'pinnies' sweep the already clean bit of pavement in front of their stolid old terraces and pronounce the last 'g' when they wish passers-by 'Good morning'. This original bit of Tynemouth huddles behind the really grand old terraces, which stand bravely facing out over the cliff tops and beaches to the North Sea beyond.

Gleaming bay windows blink and sparkle as they keep an aloof but paternal eye on tourists and locals who clutch jackets with one hand and hats with the other, as they try to admire the impressive seascape while simultaneously beating into a prevailing wind that sometimes drops below gale force on a nice day. The men invariably dress in sensible Harris tweed jackets over sensible button-up cardigans and muted paisley ties. The ladies settle for sensible windcheaters over twin sets and floral frocks topped off with floral headscarves or clear plastic ones if they wanted to show off a new hair do. Tourists gave themselves away by flaunting open toed sandals over thick grey socks whereas the natives sensibly stayed with sturdy brogues, knowing full well that the inevitable shower would soon have them racing, on smugly dry feet, for the warmth and shelter of The Gibraltar Rock, a picture postcard pub that gets more visitors than the ancient priory a hundred yards away.

North Shields on the other hand was always the poor relation and it wasn't till I sat down to relive my youth, that it dawned on me just how small the town really was. Tynemouth to the east, Percy Main to the west, New York to the North and even South Shields on the other side of the river, were all within a comfortable mile and a half of the town centre. Little wonder therefore that we kids traversed every square foot of it at one time or another or that I could still find my way around blindfolded in a fog even after an absence of forty odd years. During this time, the town has undergone some superficial changes. The old library stands empty, black and derelict, replaced with a modern version that has everything except the beautiful musty smell of the original. Some of the older, and seemingly indestructible rows of terraces that survived untold years of boisterous families, harsh elements and Hitler's bombs, have finally succumbed to progress. The council even had the temerity to rename some of the less fashionable streets in a vain attempt to upgrade the tarnished image of socially deprived areas like The Ridges Estate. Silkeys Lane, where I spent most

Tynemouth Priory.

of my childhood, has survived this programme of gentrification, but Laburnum Avenue where I lived as a young adult is now a rather grand Dorking Avenue. Even worse, Briarwood Avenue, where I delivered papers, is now (shudder) Barmouth Way. Happily, the renaming seems to have met with little success. A recently revisited Laburnum showed it to be a mess of boarded-up windows, stripped roofs, overgrown and weed-infested gardens strewn with litter, broken glass and dog poop. Not much different to the old days, come to think of it.

But that is today. The Shields of our childhood was a grimy, noisy, smelly, lively, friendly, industrious town. Its largely working class inhabitants manned the nearby collieries, sailed the merchantmen or fishing fleet that plied in and out of harbour and toiled in the shipbuilding and repair yards that stretched the length of the river. The town was surrounded by small mining communities, each with its Co-op store, its working men's club and the rows of tiny miners' cottages, grimly dark on the outside but polished and glowing and warm and hospitable once you crossed over the lovingly rubbing stoned front step. The streets quiet and often deserted apart from the odd group of night workers, crouched on their 'honkers' like so many resting crows all black and convivial as they enjoyed a smoke and a crack before the time came for them to head home to prepare for their shift 'down by'. Overshadowing the village, and the lives of its residents, was the pithead with its distinctive winding gear and the huge slagheaps that rose like barren miniature mountains from the flat surrounding countryside.

And always, there was the incessant clanging and clanking of the overhead conveyors as the black and rusted tubs carried a seemingly endless supply of coal to some distant collection point while the empties clanked and rocked by them on the return trip. In the green fields below, cows grazed, horses pulled ploughs, farmers tended crops of potatoes, cabbages and turnips, seemingly oblivious to the overhead sounds and movements that were as much a part of the landscape as the bird calls from the surrounding hedges.

Preston Colliery where my Granda McDonald and my uncles all worked, was our last local pit. I'd sit enthralled as they'd relate how they always walked to work in a group to avoid the hungry unemployed hard cases who waylaid the unwary to relieve them of their bread and cheese 'piece'. How some of them worked up to their waists in freezing water in shafts that extended for miles under the North Sea, and how they didn't start to get paid until they'd completed their long and arduous hike to the pit face. Many of them lost their lives in accidents, or even worse, from the debilitating lung diseases which they accepted stoically as a hard but inevitable part of the job. I guess they took some personal satisfaction from knowing that each bag they sweated and slaved over provided a few more pence towards keeping the Duke of Northumberland in the manner to which he and his heirs and successors had become accustomed.

Preston Colliery had drawn its last ton of coal by the time I was around but it left a great legacy in the shape of the slag heap which stood behind the playing fields of what was then Tynemouth High School. At the first real snow fall, its slatey grey slopes were magically converted into our very own Swiss Alps as an endless stream of kids trudged from near and far dragging sledges, planks of wood, corrugated iron sheets, or any other conveyance they could lay their hands on. Our battered old sledge was stored in the coal house which wasn't a problem if coal stocks were low but required a great deal of digging and pulling if we'd just had a delivery. By the time we'd extricated the sledge, removed the worst deposits of rust and coal dust and headed off for the snow fields, bunches of happy and red faced kids, who had by now turned our pristine slopes into a slushy mixture of brown icy clarts, were trudging in the opposite direction. So we'd end up fighting over who'd get the first go through the icy muck before fighting over whose turn it was to drag the sledge back on the long slow return to the coal house. It was never like that in *Nanook of the North*.

While the rich veins of coal provided the energy that fed the furnaces and stoked the boilers, the slowly running River Tyne was the artery that pumped the very lifeblood of our town and those others that sent their terraces sloping and curving along the riverside like so many industrial tea plantations.

It gradually narrows as it heads inland to Newcastle and the rugged Northumbrian countryside beyond, surely one of the most beautiful and least visited counties in all England. One Australian I knew, who was smart enough to stay a while instead of galloping through for the

Preston Colliery in the 1940s.

compulsory three days in Scotland, stopped off at a tiny Geordie mining town. Bowling into one of those tiny newsagents where the bell clangs as you pushed the door, he was served by a whizzened old local who listened incredulously to his request for a picture postcard of the said town. Carefully removing his cap, the shopkeeper scratched his head in wonderment before opinioning, 'Whey man I can't think of anybody who'd want a postcard of this place.'

We Shields folk were never as backward as that because we had a shop on Saville Street, just between the Comedy Theatre and the green bus stop which sold musical instruments including the 'submarines' that we 'doot de dooted' on.

They also had racks of sheet music for Lily of Laguna plus a terrific range of sepia postcards with pictures of the Wooden Dolly, the South Shields Ferry, and stuff like that, all nicely inscribed 'with best wishes from North Shields.' I don't know who ever bought them as there weren't any tourists in those days and its unlikely that they would have come to Shields even if there had been. But if they had, and if there'd been anything as unlikely as a conducted tour of the township, then it would almost certainly have started on top of the crumbly cliffs just inside the mouth of the river. Here, next to the Coastguard's station, high above the rocky but sheltered Tynemouth Haven, stands our monument to Admiral Lord Collingwood, a famous local lad who, on October 21st 1805, led the British Fleet into action at the Battle of Trafalgar. His statue, on its imposing column, was erected some forty years later by a grateful community, and here he still stands, head erect, calmly admiring the peaceful and ever-changing panorama below him.

The Collingwood Monument.

To his left, the river widens as it ebbs and flows between the long twin piers, each with its sturdy stone lighthouse, into a North Sea that can be brilliant calm ultramarine blue one day, a sullen swollen grey the next and a terrifying frenzy of pounding waves smashing over the high pier walls the next. Behind him the Priory points its ruined finger to the skies, while straight below lie the Black Middens a clump of unimpressively dark low rocks which all but disappear below water level at high tide and which trapped many an unwary vessel in bygone days. My Uncle Alex, who I trusted implicitly, told me that the rocks weren't rocks at all but droppings from a herd of circus elephants, held on a ship that anchored there many years ago. I think I was inclined to believe him at the time but in hindsight it seems more than likely that they were formed by normal geological processes.

A well-trod path heads inland from the monument and after a short but undulating walk brings you to the Knott's Flats. Stood, five or six stories high, this plain and utilitarian block of flats, with its walkways along each floor, afforded million dollar views to those on the riverside

The Sir James Knott Memorial Flats.

of the building and not so great views of Tynemouth railway station and the number two bus to those on the other. My mate Billy Ray had a Granny or some other relative living there and we often made the half hour hike, not because the relatives were particularly popular but because this gave us some sort of excuse to yell up the echoing stair wells, spit off the higher floors and, even better, to ride in the lifts when they were working. These creaking clanking conveyances were one of the modern mechanical miracles of the day and Billy and I would press buttons and jerk our way up to the top floor while looking as if we understood the half scrubbed out anatomical drawings on the once painted walls and bravely ignoring the fact that the interior smelled even worse than the dank little sandstone toilet block across the road. Eventually some little old lady, panting under a heavy load of shopping, would fling the folding doors open as we went down to ground level for the umpteenth time. Abusing us for having kept her waiting, she'd demand to know where we came from before threatening us with 'the polis', her threats that 'she new our Ma' following us as we took to our heels and the safety (and sweet fresh air) of the bank top.

Our escape route took us straight down the high grassy banks to the Fish Quay Sands, a small narrow expanse of beach which, as its name suggests, lies just to the seaward side of the fish quay. It's a pretty sorry little beach really, but to us kids it provided a narrow strip of sand and a calm and shallow stretch of water which was at least available, unlike the tantalisingly beautiful coastal expanses that sat mined and barbed wired for most of our childhood. It did tend to suffer from a couple of minor drawbacks. Tippy toeing over the slippery weed covered rocks that lined the water's edge wasn't too bad but it was a tad off-putting when you bumped into a floating cod's head just as you were splashing your way to tackling the thirty foot croc like Johnny Weisemuller did in the previous Saturday's Tarzan film. This, however, was considered to be a relatively small price to pay as things were even worse on those days when you arrived to find the entire stretch submerged beneath a particularly high tide. In this event, we'd clamber around what was left of the Black Middens or chuck stones at the water rats who'd sit fat and sleek on the retaining wall, daring us to hit them before sliding under the oily surface with barely a ripple to mark their departure.

Lying furiously about how many we'd killed the last time we were here and how we'd only missed that last one by half an inch, we'd meander away from the delights of the Fish Quay Sands to the bottom of the less delightful Tanners Bank. It was so named after the blackened, ugly and decrepit kipper houses that lined either side of the steep cobbled bank like so many huge beached hulks stuck high and dry in bare weed-infested yards. A perpetual wisp of smoke wafted wearily from the vents in their rusted corrugated iron roofs and through the gaps in the loose blackened planks that flapped listlessly in the breeze.

In later years, I often wondered if any of the English gentry, lying abed in their stately homes, sipping their Earl Grey and partaking of their traditional kipper breakfast, ever gave a passing thought to the poor souls who spent five and six days a week in those draughty cheerless sheds turning the freshly landed herring into that golden

Haggie's factory and the Willington Viaduct.

delicacy. The girls who laboured away in these smoke-filled hovels
were generally considered to be a bit on the rough side (although never
as tough as those legendary ladies who manned Haggie's rope factory
at Howdon). But they always seemed to me to be a boisterously
cheerful mob as they clumped around in their wellies, a chattering
screeching throng of thick jumpers bright headscarves, red faces and
cigarette smoke, their linking forearms permanently stained the same
colour as the kippers they prepared.

Those who struggled up the steeply sloping Tanners Bank were
rewarded when their wobbly legs finally brought them to more level
terrain and to Northumberland Park, a cool leafy oasis that neatly
separated the bottom end of Shields from the top end of Tynemouth.

One of our more splendid parks it was a vision of well-tended flower
beds, lawns and shrubberies all bisected by a narrow babbling brook
that ran from one end to the other. Quiet and peaceful, it provided
sanctuary to the old couples who sat silently chewing on their gums as
they carefully inspected passers-by while studiously ignoring each
other. Then there were the young mothers wrestling high prams and
rosy-cheeked babies around the tracks that wound their way up and
down and around the park. And of course there was always the

Northumberland Park at the turn of the century.

ubiquitous Parkie. Every park, no matter how modest, had to have its own Parkie. Even our nearby Storers Park which was basically a smallish paddock of straggly weeds, two concrete sand pits and a set of swings, had its own Parkie. Usually wiry little old men with toothbrush moustaches, their uniform consisted of black shiny shoes, black shiny pants, a black shiny waistcoat and a peaked council cap that established their authority just as surely as any judge's wig.

Operating from their neat little wooden huts, they patrolled their domain, a hessian bag in one hand and a stick with a nail in the end in the other, ever vigilant for any young miscreants who might look as if they were enjoying themselves or even worse for any who dared to place as much as a toe on the lawns from which DO NOT WALK ON THE GRASS signs sprouted like so many cast iron toadstools. The stick doubled as a paper picker-upper and a sergeant major's pacing stick and no Brigade of Guards RSM was ever treated with more fear and respect than these doughty guardians of each council oasis. These were undoubtedly the forefathers of the little old blokes who guard council parking areas today.

SECTION TWO

CANNY OLD SHIELDS
THE BOTTOM END

Fishermen fitting floats on the net of a North Shields trawler at the Fish Quay.

We usually avoided the park and the Parkie by utilising one of the narrow sets of steps that wound their way up between the equally grimy buildings that overlooked the Fish Quay.

Each sandstone step was worn into a smooth gentle curve and the sun never seemed to penetrate into these man-made canyons. On either side of them, small offices and trading houses sheltered like so many smugglers' caves, there only light being the feeble yellow globes that gave them a mysterious and secretive atmosphere as if they were running some sort of clandestine activity that wouldn't stand the bright examining light of day. We kids were absolutely certain that at least one of these dingy little cells sheltered shaven-headed Nazi spies who, even as we passed, were crouched over morse keys sending off coded signals to The Fatherland. Convinced we'd uncover them one day, we'd peer through filthy cracked windows or poke our heads around any half open door but all we ever unearthed were a collection of dungaree-clad men each sucking alternately on a soggy half inch Woodbine or an equally soggy half inch stub of pencil as they laboured over thick leather-bound ledgers or did convoluted sums in longhand on scraps of paper not much bigger than bus tickets. Most who spotted us hardly bothered to look up as they threatened to 'kick our arses if we didn't bugger off' but you did get the odd sadist who pretended to jump up and chase us as he roared out his warning. Screaming and terror stricken, hearts pounding and lungs pumping, we'd scale the remaining steps two at a time, jostling and pushing and pulling at each other until we finally broke back into the sunlight and the safety of the bank top.

Here the traumas of the uphill chase were quickly forgotten as we caught our breath, cooled our sweaty faces against the cast iron railings and admired the High Light, a magnificent white painted edifice which must have provided breathtaking views from its elevated vantage point. Even from its base, the vista was impressive enough as we rested long enough to review our progress so far.

Back to our left, the north and south piers stretched like two arms across the river entrance with each hand clutching the later lighthouses that had turned the High Light and the Low Light below into picturesque but redundant guardians. High on his column, Collingwood was still admiring the view to the south, the Knott's flats still stood four square above the Black Middens and the grey river still flowed past the Fish Quay Sands to the deep blue of the sea beyond.

The view, if you turned your back on this splendid scene, wasn't quite as splendid. Dockwray Square, built in the latter part of the eighteenth century, was a fine three-sided collection of grand three and four storey houses surrounding a large green. Commanding magnificent views from their huge bay windows and elevated garrets, these great edifices housed the local shipowners and doctors and

Dockwray Square, circa 1950.

clergymen and merchants and I still can't understand what possessed them to give up such a prime and prestigious position. But give it up they did, and by the 1930s they housed the poorest of the town's poor. The formerly green quadrangle was by then a desolate pock-marked desert dotted with hardy purple thistles and weeds in the dry, and a drab swampland of muddy rubbish-filled holes in the wet. The buildings themselves had degenerated into dirty and dismal slums, their dark and cavernous entrances leading to bare unswept stairs which in turn led to even barer flats within. Bunches of ragged and snotty-nosed kids sat on unscrubbed steps watching their older brothers and sisters skipping or playing among the debris while tired mothers in shabby jumpers, voluminous skirts and pinnies leaned on railings that had once subdivided neat little gardens as they caught up with the latest neighbourhood gossip.

A ninety degree turn from the sorry squalor of Dockwray Square brought a far more bustling and stirring sight into view – The Shields Fish Quay! Surely the most exciting place in the whole wide world, especially when the fishing fleet was in and the whole place a frenzy of activity.

Trawlermen bellowed from within the dark confines of congested holds as they shovelled the slippery, silvery, tail-slapping herring into wicker crans. Steaming winches, swung and lifted them to the quayside where their contents poured like quicksilver into the smooth slimy crates in which they'd be transported the length and breadth of the country. These actions were replicated on trawler after trawler after trawler until the scene became a blur of bobbing boats, swaying masts, swinging winches, banging trolleys and yelling men. Trawlers from Shields and Grimsby and Lowestoft and Hull and Leith and Aberdeen and Bergen and a host of other ports, all sturdy practical solid little craft dull and rusted and uniformly drab, embellished only by the rich

Landing the catch at the Fish Market.

scrolling painted around their usually female names. Labourers dragged trolleys piled with empty crates onto the quayside as fast as their mates pushed their heavily laden ones off. 'Omo' white seagulls scrawked and wheeled in great flocks, swooping and fighting over the tiddlers dislodged from nets and thrown into the cold grey waters that lapped leadenly against the wooden hulls. Battered trucks tooted and honked and struggled their way through the crush, wheels sliding, gears crashing and engines screaming as they jockeyed to pick up the cod and herring and mackerel and skate and flounder before renegotiating themselves back from whence they'd come.

Despite the black curved roof that covered two thirds of the quayside everything was always cold and wet! Wet from the fish that slipped and

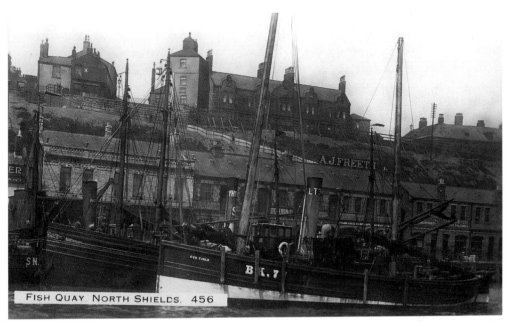

The Fish Quay.

Union Quay east of the Fisherman's Mission, near to where Hastie's fish shop is now.

slopped everywhere, wet from the huge hoses that cleaned decks and walkways with great spouting jets of river water, wet from the ice in which the fish were bedded down for their onward journey, and often as not, wet from the grey drizzle that crept softly in from the sea when you least expected it. The workers all bundled up in oilskins, rubber thighboots and layers of cable stitched woollen jumpers seemed impervious to the freezing conditions, though closer examination revealed hands reddened and chapped from the long hours spent foraging through their icebound produce. Trawlermen easily recognisable by their once white polo necked jumpers and their rolling gait, left the mundane clearing up tasks to their poor shorebound cousins as they set off for home and family, their newspaper wrapped free 'fry', clutched firmly in callused hands. And always on the fringes of all of this activity were the lookers-on. The oldies out for their constitutional, the drifters and unemployed looking for a few hours 'busking', the local polis leaning on his bike as he kept an aloof and benevolent eye on proceedings, the traders and hanger-ons and of course, us kids.

Eventually the bustle would abate. Unenthusiastic sweepers wielding wide-bristled brooms methodically built soggy piles of rubbish that blew away before they could pick them up. Men in huge leather aprons hosed off the fish scales and stacked great towers of smelly crates ready for the next onslaught, while others in dark sloppy sheds and workshops, wielded razor sharp knives with the dexterity of brain

A trawler at the Fish Quay shed.

surgeons as they beheaded and cut and scaled and filleted tomorrow's fish dinners. Mangey cats sniffed around bins of stinking offal, totally ignoring the swarms of glistening turquoise bluebottles that buzzed and hummed and fed and multiplied. Now the odd amateur fisherman sat on satin-smooth iron bollards to which some trawler had so recently been tied, his heavy cord line unmoving testament to the fact that the only fish around here were in boxes. Kids dangling cods' heads on lengths of twine had more success dragging in the small crabs that refused to release their grip till the very last minute when they opened their claws and flopped back down to their submarine homes. The odd maintenance man hammered or welded or sawed but there seemed to be little enthusiasm for any of these tasks which merely marked time until the real action started again. Meanwhile, the local craft rested, battened down and deserted. Crews of visiting craft alongside them, whiled away the hours cosily ensconced within the tight confines of the bridge drinking treacle like tea out of chipped tin mugs or lounged on the after deck enjoying the last weak rays of sunlight as they chatted and repaired nets with a dexterity that any embroidress would have envied. Conversation centred around the weather, what time they'd sail in the morning, what was the best pub considering that the beer round here was like maiden's water and not a patch on the stuff at home wherever that might be. Soon depending on tides and owners

Net mending on trawlers at Union Quay.

Anglers on the quay.

Cleaning fish at Tyne Brand.

schedules, each craft would cast off the thick hawsers that provided their temporary link to the shore. Resting seagulls screeched off to view the action from safer vantage points as smoke billowed, engines chugged to life and the calm waters churned as each craft slowly manoeuvred out of the gut and into the mainstream. Here they'd follow those ahead, black triangular sails set and bows digging deeper and deeper as the swell built up and they pushed their blunt noses into the darkening sea and the fishing grounds beyond.

The short walk from Dockwray Square to the Harbour View was best carried out at a brisk trot because, frankly, this was not the most scenic quarter mile in North Shields.

The steeply sloping bank on the left was a weed-infested wasteland of derelict, blackened and rusted old buildings, their broken windows a mute testimony to the stone throwing abilities of the local toughs. The quay below gave way to the ice works, a small shipyard and of course the almost mandatory pub. This particular pub distinguished by the fact that, just outside its front door, at the end of a darkly forbidding alleyway, stood one of Shields' most famous landmarks, the Wooden Dolly.

The ice factory from the Tyne.

In years past, the streets of Shields had been trodden by generations of fishwives who peddled their laden crans from door to door. This life-sized replica perfectly captured the spirit of these hardy women. Dressed in long skirts and voluminous petticoats, the heavy basket held one-handed on one shoulder as she leaned forward to trudge her way up and down the cobbled streets hoping to make the few pence that would keep the wolf from the door for just a few more days. If the Mona Lisa was enigmatic then our local work of art was positively mysterious. This was due in no small part to the fact that some local

The fourth Wooden Dolly.

vandal, for reasons known only to himself, had neatly chopped off Dolly's face. This never bothered us as we struggled to climb her back and sit aside her cran with legs lolling over her tireless shoulders. She has since been replaced by at least one updated and multi-coloured version, complete with face but to me, the Wooden Dolly will always be the cracked and weathered old faceless timber version that guarded the entrance to the alleyway that went nowhere.

The top of the bank at this point matched the squalor of the buildings below. This old section of town was always, even in the rosiest of my memories, uniformly grey, drab and neglected, the only two bright spots being the IOGT and the undertakers. The Independent Order of Good Templars, or 'I Owe Ganny Tuppence' as it was more generally known was a sort of temperance type Sunday School where I went a few times with my cousin Maureen who used to sing 'In My Sweet Little Alice Blue Gown' at their concerts or parties or services or whatever they were. I can't, for the life of me, see what possible relevance this might have had towards encouraging us to forsake a life of drunkenness and debauchery but I must admit that the oath we took to neither touch, taste nor handle alcoholic liquor certainly seemed to work as I don't recall touching a drop as long as I went there. Just around the corner from the IOGT stood the darkest, dustiest and dingiest little undertakers shop outside a Charles Dickens novel. The front window was the only part of the premises that ever carried a skerrick of paint. Whitewashed, countless years before to keep prying eyes away from the even grottier interior, it was now a scratched and nondescript creamy colour which blended nicely with the flaking and

Fishwives at Bennett's in the 1930s.

indeterminately colourless timber surrounds. Sheer terror prevented me from ever seeing the inside of what looked like a film set for a Frankenstein movie but, like most every other kid who passed, I had peered through the scratches in the window and yelled 'Got any old boxes?' before fleeing for the safety of Howard Street. Although I never saw anything more threatening than a dust-covered counter and a few bits and pieces of lumber, there were plenty other kids prepared to swear that they'd seen tons of bodies standing in coffins all around the walls. These were almost certainly the same kids who always saw the nun's ghost in the bombed church at the bottom of Borough Bank.

Just past the undertakers was a blackened old sandstone building that was battened and closed up for as long as I could remember. I do have this very early recollection however of being taken there by Wor Ma when I must have been only three or four years old. Don't ask me what happened at Bishopsgate House or who did what there but I think it was a sort of meeting place for young mothers and their children because I remember sitting among a crowd of similar aged kids watching my very first pantomime. I guess it would have been a pretty home-made sort of production and, as far as I know as it didn't star John Mills or anyone else who'd go on to fame and stardom. But it did contain one magical theatrical scene that has stayed with me for over sixty years. A fair damsel had got herself into a bit of bother and was waving her arms and giving a pretty convincing impression of drowning in the middle of the perfectly dry stage. Luckily our hero, who just happened to be passing by, saw her plight and, to our relieved cheers, vowed to dive in and save her … just as soon as he took off his new pullover. So off came the pullover as our heroine screamed and waved and went down for the umpteenth time. Then came another pullover and a jumper and a cardigan and another pullover then another and yet another till the stage was strewn with what seemed to me like hundreds of pullovers and a still screaming and waving heroine. Over the ensuing years, I've seen just about everything from *Oklahoma* to *Miss Saigon* but nothing that went even close to matching that amazing multi-pullovered scene.

Bishopgate House's huge double doors led straight to the bottom of Howard Street and a choice of routes for us tourists. A turn to the right led straight up a slight hill past, on the right, the old Bainbridge's Sale Rooms whose bare wooden floors Wor Ma used to scrub for about two bob an acre. This was a handy spot to stop and fossick if you'd just missed a bus or if you were on the lookout for a mangle or a five bob Persian carpet all the way from Macclesfield. Directly opposite stood our much-loved public library on the corner of Saville Street, our premiere thoroughfare that ran past the Post Office and Police Station on the right and through the main shopping centre on the left.

This should not be confused with that other Saville Row which is in

Saville Street in the 1940s.

Woolworth's in Saville Street West.

A North Shields lady at home in the 1930s.

London or somewhere although this would be a perfectly excusable mistake to make as our fine collection of shops included Moore's where Wor Ma always did her grocery shopping, Todd's where an early girlfriend sold hats that were so posh they called them millenary, a Woolworth's that boasted 'nothing over threepence or sixpence' and a penny dip shop that served the best pork dips in the world. Then there was a public toilet with nice wrought iron railings, a little butchers shop that sold vile looking whale meat during the war, a furniture store where I bought this lovely plaster parrot for Wor Ma one Christmas, a number of tobacconists who somehow survived years without having anything to sell plus a 'Polis Box' where belligerent drunks got their wallops on a Saturday night. I've never had the pleasure of seeing the other Saville Row but it seems extremely unlikely that it could ever have matched the grandeur and diversity of this elegant concourse.

The top half of Howard Street, after it crossed Saville Street, carried straight on up to Northumberland Square, the real centre of the town where all the buses started and stopped, where the posh people visited their solicitors and us poor folk sneaked into the offices of T. Archer Lee to take 'a ticket'. In these days before credit cards or hire purchase, T. Archer Lee was literally our 'ticket' to a new suit, a pair of shoes, a bike, a few yards of lino, a set of tools or whatever other luxury took our parent's fancy. The system was simple and straightforward. You tackled the three or four nice clean sandstone steps, pushed open the door which had T. Archer Lee tastefully inscribed in gold leaf, went through a second frosted glass door to where an all-seeing and all-knowing lady did the paperwork and kept a mental list of every bad debt within a ten mile radius. Most folk easily passed her probity test because they'd been coming here for years and had probably just finished paying off their last ticket. In this case she'd open her little duplicate book which looked a bit like a set of raffle tickets for the Irish Sweepstake. Then she'd enter your name, write in the name of the local store where you intended to spend the dough then fill in the amount you wanted to borrow. In return, all you had to do was to come back every week for a full year to pay off fifty week's worth of debt plus two weeks profit for T. Archer Lee. Only the desperately poor and near-destitute used the resources of this firm which accounts for the fact that they had more names on their rolls than the local council.

Howard Street and the Square were old people's territory and us young 'uns would almost certainly have avoided it by heading instead to the Harbour View. This ugly two-tiered concrete lookout at the bottom end of Howard Street, was almost certainly designed by the same bloke who built Hitler's bomb shelter. A stolid dull concrete edifice, its lower level a cold toilet like place where the wind whipped the dust and fag ends around the legs of the cast iron benches that nobody ever sat on. We didn't have proper graffiti because spray cans hadn't been invented and most folk couldn't afford paint for the walls of their houses let alone the walls of the Harbour View and this was a shame because a bit of colourful graffiti might have just brightened the place up a bit. Wor Ma always double warned us keep away from here because it was a well known fact that the notorious Dirty Dick and Tommy Noddy hung around here all the time. I'm not sure how we were supposed to recognise them as nobody seemed to know exactly what either of these world famous perverts looked like. To be on the safe side, we avoided any possible confrontation by always galloping through the bottom section and up the stairs to the street level where obviously harmless little old men sat quietly smoking the sort of clay pipes that we used to blow soap bubbles through. The lookout at this level was still pretty unimpressive but not so the view it commanded. Miles of river snaked left to the piers or right to Jarrow and Wallsend and beyond. Straight opposite, the terraces of our sister town criss-crossed the terrain much like ours except ours was far more attractive because even we kids knew that South Shields wasn't a patch on North Shields and that all the people over there were soft as clarts.

Just fifty yards away from the Harbour View, on the corner of Union Street, stood D. Hill Carter an ancient store and one of those rock-solid institutions which sold just about everything and from which just about everybody had bought something at one time or another. Its huge display windows stretched along both street frontages, in a stupefyingly dull display of utterly boring items. Drab rolls of linoleum in varying shades of green and brown stood next to more expensive carpets which were draped to show off the equally drab greys and browns which may not have brightened the family hearth but were guaranteed 'not to show the dirt'. Stiff male dummies with chipped noses and missing fingers stood woodenly in other windows, each carefully bedecked in bib and brace overalls or boiler suits or dungarees, each in a stunning range of navy blue and black. The women's window was by far the most colourful and the models seemed slightly less chipped but just as wooden as they posed purposefully, one arm elegantly outstretched, dainty index finger extended as they showed off the latest fashion in floral frocks, floral skirts and floral pinnies. The models all had that yellow crinkly wavy hair-do that might have looked OK on Clara Bow but that looked more like corrugated iron on the porcelain dummies.

It was here every spring that the four of us were dragged by Wor Ma for the annual fit out ready for the Good Friday March.

Pushing through the twelve foot high double doors was more like entering a cathedral than a store. From here on in, everything was done at a whisper as we crept like a bunch of condemned prisoners over the sloping polished floors, through the polished arches till we came to the children's department where stunted porcelain models with angelic expressions and more yellow hair pointed accusingly at us as we awaited the attention of any one of the highly starched shop assistants who followed our every step, subconsciously daring one of us to so much as lay a finger on anything we weren't supposed to. With this preliminary examination out of the way, the head assistant would nod almost imperceptibly at our designated assistant, usually a lady, who then detached herself from whatever she was dusting and stepped up to Wor Ma who handed across her T. Archer Lee ticket while explaining quietly what she required. This brief routine immediately established what garments were wanted for whom and, more importantly and exactly to the penny, how much she had to spend on these items.

The selection process was made easier for all concerned as we simply observed the three golden rules of fashion that applied universally at that time. Rule one stated that all outer garments be either grey, black or navy blue. Rule two decreed that nothing new should fit comfortably while rule three ensured that all trousers must have huge baggy behinds. Doctors, lawyers, poets, peasants, kings and commoners alike were all destined to go through life wearing pants that only ever touched their individual bums when they sat down. Being the eldest I was usually the first to be ministered to by the big bosomed lady who expertly assessed me as size eight before trotting off to get a size twelve on the basis that, 'I'd soon grow into it.' We kids didn't justify anything as sophisticated as changing rooms but nobody seemed to notice as we slipped out of well loved grey pants that fitted and wrestled into the new ones that were so stiff they could have stood up on their own. Then followed a convoluted wrestling match as you and the assistant struggled to force the metal buttons through buttonholes that traditionally were just a millimetre or two smaller than the discs they were supposed to accommodate. Finally, all red faced and breathless, the lady stood triumphantly, grabbed a great handful of surplus seat and tugged the whole lot backwards so that the three or four inches of slack in the waistline temporarily disappeared into her great fist, as she hoisted me on tip toes and spun me to face the mirror. I could see the same doubts in Wor Ma's eyes as in mine as I viewed myself almost buried in these great grey sacks that couldn't quite make up their mind whether they were long shorts of short longs. Even the mildest of protests were brushed aside as our 'helper' proudly proclaimed that not only would you never get a better fit but that additionally they wouldn't show the dirt and finally how I would grow into them. Powerless against such super salesmanship and such irrefutable logic, the evidence of our own eyes was dismissed as the pants headed for the counter where they'd shortly be joined by all the other grey oversized purchases as my brothers Brian and Derek took

The Christenson family in all their Easter finery, circa 1942. Left to right: Norman, Brian, Derek and Doreen.

their turns. Little girls didn't seem to be subjected to the same indignities so I'm not sure how my sister Doreen got her stuff. Our final move was to the leathery smelling shoe department, where an equally leathery old man forced feet into shoes that were as stiff and unyielding as a Papal bull.

Like the pants, the shoes were always two or three sizes too big with the result that each of us lurched up and down the test carpet strip like Frankenstein's monster on skis as our fitter ooh'd and aah'd and told Ma how lucky we were to get such a good fit first time around. The best and most exciting part of this annual pilgrimage was still to come. As Wor Ma stood tense and watchful, our assistant painstakingly licked

Union Stairs off Liddle Street, leading up to D. Hill Carter.

his or her pencil and laboriously added the various purchases together till finally they arrived at a total that, miraculously, was always just within the limits of the ticket. Sometimes there was even a little bit left over and one of us, usually me, got an extra treat in the shape of a scarf or a pair of gloves till all of the ticket was used up. Then and only then, the ticket and all the calculations were placed in a small screw capped container which in turn was attached to a series of overhead lines that whisked them away to points unknown where hidden staff double checked the bill before sending it back with maybe a few pence change. The sight of these egg shaped containers whizzing from one end of the store to the other was a source of constant amazement to all of us who left the store quietly wondering how modern science could ever top such an outstanding example of high technology.

In direct contrast, Stagg and Son on the other corner diagonally opposite was a very different sort of shop. Operated by a father and son team, Staggies as they were known to all and sundry, could well have been the Geordie forerunners of Steptoe and son. One of the pair, usually the son, trundled a handcart around town, yelling 'rags and bones'. I don't know why he did this because I never saw a bone on that cart as long as it traversed the County Borough of Tynemouth, picking up pre-loved heirlooms for anything up to a hard fought thruppence. These objets d'art were then transported back to the store where the old man sat on guard just inside the double doors, hunched down in a great black horse hair filled chair, puffing on the last half inch of a cigarette. Behind him, the sagging mildewed ceiling and flaking walls encompassed mounds of merchandise that customers were forced to examine via a maze of passageways that meandered hither and thither like a game trail through the African veldt. Chairs with broken legs leaned drunkenly against mouldy couches whose cushions barely hid protruding springs. A grandfather clock which once graced a far more stately home now stood dusty and dejected, its shoulders bowed over a collection of battered alarm and mantle clocks that all showed different times and were all well past their last tick. Hand-operated sewing machines propped up rusted bicycles with flat tyres and spokes that protruded like the blades on Boadicea's chariot while the 'tool section' carried an amazing array of shovels without handles, axes that looked as though they'd just hacked their way through the concrete jungle and cardboard boxes full of nuts and bolts none of which ever went together. Stags with moth-eaten coats and lustreless glass eyes looked down on misted glass domes from which owls and hawks gazed unblinkingly at a stuffed ferret that had long ceased to represent any sort of a threat. Piles of dishes and jugs and plates and cups and saucers and china ornaments, some of them still in one piece, cluttered sideboards and dressers and tables while every available corner had teetering towers of pots and pans and skillets and

Stagg's Shop on the corner of Union Street and Bedford Street.

trays that once held a tasty family treat but were now the last resting place of hundreds of dead flies. A large shallow bowl in one window carried a tangle of wire-framed spectacles while next to it, a dusty willow patterned plate carried an impressive collection of yellowing false teeth. Chunky china uppers mixed with smiling lower sets, all obviously no longer needed by their owners who had either upgraded or gone on to that great dentist in the sky. I never saw anyone trying them out for size and to give the Staggs due credit, they never stooped to modern sales techniques by describing them as 'hardly used' or 'one custard-eating owner only'. Whatever happened to all these treasures when Staggies closed their doors for the last time remains one of life's little mysteries although I suspect the British Museum could well have been a major beneficiary.

Our upriver trek took us from Staggies past a pub where my Dad went to some secret society called 'The Buffaloes' and across the bottom of Bedford Street where my Grandma Mac lived in one of a row of really ancient cottages when I must have been very young. The combination of tiny windows and heavy curtains turned the cell-like living-room into a dank dark cave, destined never to see or feel the warmth of the sun. While these conditions may have been less than ideal for humans, they were absolutely perfect for the other residents. As you entered the perpetual darkness of the room, the walls were a seething mass of what we called black beetles but which were probably small cockroaches. As soon as a match was struck and the gas lamp lit, they disappeared as if by magic into the lath and plaster walls where they hid and bred until the light was dowsed once more. What, in later years, struck me as really remarkable about this was, that at the time, everyone seemed to accept the vanishing act as being quite normal and unremarkable.

Just across the road stood the Evangelistic Mission, a tiny church which stood below an even tinier pub that you entered via a sort of drawbridge. It was probably the only church in Shields that smelled better than the Newcastle Brewery. Fifty yards down the hill, the Tiger Stairs climbed from the steeply cobbled Lower Bedford Street to a pretty nondescript bit of the town filled with nondescript terraces, a few nondescript corner shops, one or two nondescript pubs and the very nondescript Boro Theatre. It would also boast, in later years, Shields' first Chinese cafe, The Canton. We never went near there firstly because it was a well known fact that it was frequented by Chinamen with razor sharp meat cleavers just like the ones in the Charlie Chan movies, and secondly because they didn't serve chips and we never ate anything without chips.

This quiet little section of town, only spitting distance below bustling Saville Street, terminated in Yeoman Street. Here perched high atop the grassy bank, the old terraces had outstanding views of the

Bedford Street.

streets and river below. And what a busy bustling view it was. Tankers, freighters, barges, passenger boats, and even the odd naval vessel puffing and smoking and steaming their way up or down stream. The larger ones pushed and pulled and prodded by the powerful tugs that coaxed and cajoled them through the traffic while the smaller ones made their own way as most of them had done many times before. And always, there were the black ugly smoky colliers, the laden ones low in the water as they wallowed their way toward the piers and their southern destinations while their equally grimy, but empty, returning sister ships, tooted and whistled their way back upstream to the staithes at Howdon and another load of coal to go the way of the tens of thousands before. Anyone with romantic notions about a life at sea under the Red Ensign on some mighty merchantman, visiting exotic ports, each of which contained an equally exotic girl would have had his expectations seriously dashed after a trip or two on these grotty tubs. Perpetually dirty, continually cold and uncomfortable, covering the same stretch of water with all the predictability of a number six bus was hardly the stuff that the likes of C. S. Forrester waxed lyrical about.

Ropery Banks West, Yeoman Street, before the Second World War.

Clive Street when Norman was a boy.

Clive Street below was a narrow old thoroughfare that ran along the rivers edge, our green grassy bank on one side and a ramshackle collection of tottering commercial buildings and small jetties on the other. It was a well known fact that one of these buildings was the headquarters of a mob of Maltese gangsters just like the ones that gave Humphrey Bogart so much trouble. God knows what any self-respecting Maltese Falcon would have got up to in those days when riding a bike without lights would have just about made the crime page of the *Shields Evening News*. Clive Street terminated at the New Quay, a small cobbled area from which overseas travellers could catch one of the two ferries that made the five minute crossing to South Shields. The smaller of these was always known as the Penny Ferry, even when the fare had inflated to a massive tuppence or threepence. A tiny little tub it couldn't have carried more than twenty or thirty bodies even if they'd stood shoulder to shoulder, unlike its big brother the Big Ferry that not only carried people but cars and trucks that would otherwise have had to make the long trip inland to Newcastle and the first bridge.

The cobbled area from which the ferries operated was also the starting point for the buses that chugged their way up Borough Bank to Saville Street, then the Square and thence to Tynemouth, Whitley Bay and the Spanish City with its dodgem cars and amusements. Some services even went to far off Blyth but we never went because it was more than five miles away and the people were even funnier than those on the other side of the river. The bus stops and ferry landings were overlooked by one of Shields' most famous landmarks, the Northumberland Arms, a forbidding blackened sandstone hostelry that was known to all and sundry as the Jungle. Infamous for its brawls and arrests and (ahem) painted ladies, the Jungle was part of our culture

P. Joyce, New Quay Post Office and the Exchange Hotel in Clive Street.

The Penny Ferry.

and no local youth had really grown up till he'd been there, been sick, been thumped in a fight he couldn't remember or chatted-up a woman old enough to be his mother. Sadly my sheltered childhood prevented me experiencing any of these alternatives and I never saw beyond the impressive front door. Many years later, I was shocked to find that it had been converted into some sort of mega trendy night club where couples sipped gin and tonics and discussed the latest stock market figures. Which only goes to show that nothing is sacred any more.

Borough Bank was traversed by a pedestrian bridge from which we used to spit on the red busses as they laboured there way up the hill at a bit under walking pace. Once over the bridge, the noise told you that you were rapidly approaching Smith's Dock. Covering acres of riverside it was enclosed by high concrete walls only slightly less impressive than the one in China that gets all the publicity. Festooned with miles of barbed wire or embedded with jagged pieces of broken glass, I always assumed as a kid that these measures were aimed at keeping intruders out. Many years later, when I joined the thousands of others who worked there, it rapidly dawned on me that in fact those elaborate and effective fortifications were designed solely to keep the poor bloody inmates inside.

And highly skilled inmates it had aplenty. Caulkers, cabinet makers, riveters, welders, painters, boilermakers, patternmakers, riggers, engineers, fitters and turners, shipwrights, draughtsmen, instrument makers, crane drivers, plumbers and a host of others. Add to them, the labourers who heated the rivets, slung the ropes, scoured the bilges, berthed the ships, made the tea and performed all the other dirty manual tasks needed to pull great ships apart and put them back together again and you had a wealth of skills and talents of which the North East was justifiably proud. And there was always the none-stop noise and activity of the place. Riveting guns hammering, welders

The Northumberland Arms, New Quay.

flashing, machines grinding and showering sparks like a Guy Fawkes'
Night display, whistles blowing and men yelling as cranes whirred and
whined and swung huge metal panels while smoke plumed and steam
hissed all in a cacophony of noise and movement. Little wonder that
my one ambition was to grow up and get through those gates to serve
my time as a shipwright. Don't ask me why a shipwright because even
today I'm not sure what shipwrights do but it had a nice ring to it and
besides everybody reckoned that fitters were ten a penny.

Those were the absolute hey-day of the ship repairing industry.
Vessels lay two or three deep awaiting there turn in the next available
dry dock. Everyone in Shields had a relative, neighbour or friend who
joined the army of workers who trudged or bused or biked to the dock
gates six days a week. The town set its clocks from the sirens that
called the faithful to work in the morning then sent them home again
at the end of the ten hour shift. Week after week, month after month
and year after year they trooped their way on pleasant summer
mornings and on long bleak wintry days when both trips started and
finished in miserable pitch black conditions made bearable only by the
fact that everyone else had to suffer them. To this generation, with their
strong sense of pride in the craftsmanship of their colleagues and in the
vessels they built and repaired, it must have seemed inconceivable that
any of this could ever change. But change it did as Unions learned the
militancy of the fifties and sixties while old and unresponsive
managements refused to learn anything at all. And so today the ships
no longer come, the sparks no longer fly, the cranes don't swing, the

riveters don't assail your ears and Shields will never again be the place it was.

So this was yesterday's Shields, not all of it of course because in addition to the main places of interest there were a thousand and one others where we lived and played and explored. There were the houses, the fields, the back lanes, the yards, the bridges, the tunnels, the gardens, the parks and so much more. The pigeon duckets hidden away behind the high walls down the Gas Yard Lane. The allotments where we went on Sunday mornings for threepen'th of rhubarb from a nice old man whose name escapes me. The lake at Tynemouth where we caught tiddlers in a net made from a Hindhaughs' flour bag and the old blackened tower that used to be Billy Mill. Northumberland Square, where as callow youths, we trotted on New Year's Eve in the hope that we might get a kiss from someone we fancied. The Billiard Hall that smelled even worse than Hadaway's fish shop below and the YMCA where we drank penny cups of tea and smoked and tried to look tough. The dip under the bridge on Waterville Road that always flooded and the drunk who responded to our cheers by swimming it in an overcoat that must have weighed a ton.

We Shield's folk were never given to boasting but all of us knew deep down inside that this just had to be the greatest place on God's earth.

A pigeon ducket between Union Street and Bedford Street.

SCHOOLDAYS

A class at Queen Victoria School, circa 1939. Norman is third from the left in the front row.

Wor Ma was forever telling us to enjoy our schooldays because they'd be the happiest days of our entire lives. Many's the time I dragged my weary feet up to the High School, the rain dripping off my nose end as I tried to work out whether I'd be in more trouble for being late, or for the undone algebra homework that was due that morning, or for the history book that I'd lost somewhere or other. And the thought often crossed my mind that if these were the happiest days of my life then I must have a hell of a lot of pain and misery ahead of me. But it wasn't always like that.

I couldn't wait to start school and I can see myself dragging Wor Ma along West Percy Road at a gallop as we marched off for my very first day at Queen Victoria Junior School. QV, all solid and square and respectable, two and a bit floors of red brick relieved only by the odd yellow blocks inset above and alongside some of the tall windows that the teachers opened and closed with great long poled hooks that may well have been used at the Battle of Agincourt. Surrounded on three sides by respectable old terraces and back lanes and on the other side of Coach Lane by the local Catholic school where kids from another planet were taught by nuns who wore coifs and long black habits that scared the living daylights out of us Protestants, more accustomed to almost human teachers in tweed skirts and tweed suits. We boys seldom got above the ground floor, the higher floors seemingly reserved for stuff like domestic science, a none too scientific subject, where the girls learned to bathe stiff porcelain dolls in tin tubs and cook exotic meals like toad in the hole and cottage pie. Sister Doreen went there later and she used to bring home stuff for the rest of us to try, but despite Wor Ma's very best warning looks and threatening headshakes, it invariably ended in tears as we three lads choked and spat and rolled on the floor clutching our throats in a manner that was clearly not intended to show our intense appreciation of her culinary efforts.

I loved QV even though you'd never guess it from the sole picture I have of our class taken when I was seven or eight years old, twenty four of us, exactly fifty-fifty boys and girls all staring suspiciously at the strange man with the big camera and the flash thing that went off with a better bang than most of the fireworks we got for Guy Fawkes' Night.

Schooling in these dark ages was light years away from today's liberated methods. It operated on some fairly simple and basic criteria, the most important of which was that we knew absolutely nothing, the teachers knew absolutely everything so if we shut up and sat there and listened for long enough there was just an outside possibility that we might learn something. Our first few years were spent 'doing our letters' on small slates and endlessly reciting our times tables in classrooms where our piping young voices bounced off the high ceilings and walls that were adorned only by the bare necessities, namely a picture of HM the King and a map of the world that rolled up into a long metal tube. No matter what time of day you passed that school you'd have heard one or more classes intoning their 'three times three is nine, four times three is twelve, five times ...' like so many Gregorian monks working their way through some ancient catechism.

It's easy to sneer at these primitive methods today when six-year-olds can sit at a computer and calculate the square root of 632 quicker than we could sharpen our pencils but it's worth remembering that this generation would one day work in shops and factories where they'd be expected to calculate the price of six ounces of best butter at one and fourpence ha'penny a pound or seven feet of fabric at seven and six a yard. Not only would they carry out these calculations while the customer stood over them purse in hand, but they'd do them with nothing more than the ubiquitous stub of pencil on the corner of the paper in which the butter or cloth or whatever was wrapped. And more often than not they'd get it right!

Our daily routine was broken two or three times a year when the district nurse bowled into the class with her surgical tray, her tooth comb and her steely-eyed determination to stamp out the head lice (dickies) that even rich kids got sometimes. Sat at the raised teacher's table, she'd glare disapprovingly at us as we all struggled to get to the back of the queue that our teacher pushed and prodded us into. The routine that followed was well established. As each kid stepped forward, nursey grasped them firmly by the upper arm with a grip that usually left five red finger prints if you stood still and five black and blue ones if you didn't. The official toothcomb was dipped into the prussic acid or whatever it was she used to sanitise it then dragged through your hair four or five times. All my life, I always wanted to have lovely curly hair, all my life, that is, except this one day when the shaved Ridges cut was a decided advantage. Not so, the poor girls and the curly tops who stood silently, teeth clenched, eyes welling as the comb snagged and pulled and tugged before finally tearing clear, its teeth clenched around handfuls of golden tresses. The offending locks were inspected minutely by the nurse. Satisfied that the comb and entangled locks were free from vermin, the victim was then waved disdainfully back to his or her seat where we all sat with burning scalps, glad to be through the ordeal and even gladder to be spared the ignominy of being handed the little slip of paper which nursey filled in with great relish for those poor kids who suffered the embarrassment of being found to be infected. I often thought afterwards that it would have been more appropriate if she'd donned a black cap whenever she filled in the dreaded dickey docket.

The tedium of times tables, letters and spelling bees was broken yet again for a far more eagerly anticipated occasion, when the junior school put on its special annual extravaganza to celebrate Empire Day. Now we kids were never brainwashed in the way we think the poor

Russians were, for example, but it's pretty clear that our educators didn't miss too many opportunities to instil in us the wonders of the British Empire. Our maps were nicely coloured so that the bits we'd conquered and civilised, like India and Canada and Australia etc, were all nicely coloured pink and we all knew that the sun never set on these mighty dominions. All of these places were looked after by the King who had heaps of palaces and long furry cloaks and crowns full of jewels and who rode on horses and even had his own train. I don't remember anybody ever telling us what the people who lived in the pink bits thought about of these arrangements as this was probably considered to be irrelevant.

Come the great day, we were across on the dew-wet front field straight after breakfast to pick fresh daisies that Wor Ma, and countless others, carefully wrapped in cigarette foil before pinning them to coats or jumpers. Then off along West Percy Road, the more excitable of us singing:

> 'Twenty fourth of May, the Queen's birthday
> If we don't get a holiday we'll all run away'

as we each tried to remember the parts we'd play in the events we'd been rehearsing for weeks previously. One year we did this fantastic gymnastic display where kids dived through hoops, walked along upside down wooden forms, skipped through ropes and, in a staggering grand finale ran at a strip of matting where we 'cowped wor kreels' (performed somersaults for none Geordie speakers) not once but twice before standing all red faced and dizzy to take our well-deserved plaudits.

As great a spectacle as this undoubtedly was, it would be put well and truly in the shade the next year when little Norman was to play a starring role in our epic tribute to the Empire. By mid-morning, the playground was a sea of faces as proud parents and grandparents were shepherded behind carefully chalked lines by bossy teachers while even bossier teachers, inside the school, prepared the cast of thousands (well at least a hundred or so anyway) for the imminent De Millian showcase. Finally everything was in place. Miss Somebody or other hammered out God Save The King on our battered old piano, four kids carefully raised the Union Jack to the top of the flagpole where it flapped proudly over the headmaster as he welcomed honoured guests and parents and declared the festivities duly opened. Now it was my turn. Swallowing nervously I marched smartly to the centre of the playground and onto the elaborate dais made from two milk crates wrapped in red, white and blue paper. A tense hush settled over the crowd as I carefully unrolled the ornate scroll off one of the two twelve inch rulers and in my poshest of posh voices started to introduce the

North Shields children pose for Empire Day.

great and colourful cavalcade. 'Welcome to our brave and noble savages from sunny, far off Tanganyika' at which a group of beaming kids marched proudly out, all wrapped in stripy cloth, their faces glowing beneath the cocoa make-up. They were followed by 'Our fearsome Ghurkha friends from afar who stood by our side in the Great War' again clad in the same striped cloth but this time waving cardboard knives in their cocoed hands. Then, 'Our proud lumberjack friends from the frozen wastes of far off Canada' this time followed by a gaggle of smug white-faced kids carrying make believe axes and dressed in tartan winter jackets and astrakhan hats. This had been one of the harder groups to outfit as most of us kids didn't have a jacket of any description let alone one of those tartan ones that any of us would have killed for. The girls and the striped cloth and cocoa got back into the act as 'We warmed our wintry British days with tea from far off Ceylon'

And so it went on till the last of the mostly brown-faced and stripy-clothed kids had marched past the dais and come to a halt facing the audience who nudged neighbours as they pointed out their very own offspring. Then Mrs What's-her-name struck up Land of Hope and Glory, we all sang as if our lungs would burst, the teachers stood proud and proprietorial, the mothers and grandmothers looked at each other and snuffled and the odd Dad sniffed and pretended he had something in his eye. The headmaster declared proceedings closed, we kids cheered and ran to receive the admiration of our parents and to walk home together for the half day holiday. It was days like this that made you proud to be British and best.

At age eight or nine we put all this show biz stuff behind us when we moved into the 'big end'. Here we had the occasional cultural day when we'd recite poems like 'Drake is in his hammock now' or sing traditional Geordie songs like 'Caa Hackie through the watter' and I was a shoemaker's elf in a play where I had to utter that most memorable line, 'You're nothing but a lazy good for nothing scamp.' I don't think it was by Shakespeare. But as our headmaster Jack Sparks was fond of reminding us, these were merely sideshows on the long hard road that led to the dreaded Grading Exam or the eleven plus as it was more often called. Under this palpably unfair system, every kid in his or her final year at primary school had to sit this exam to determine the next step in their education.

Those who finished in the top hundred or so were eligible to move on to Tynemouth's sole high school where they'd study languages and the advanced subjects needed to qualify for university or other tertiary institutions. The remaining ninety percent who 'failed' the exam moved on to one or the other of the town's two secondary schools where the courses were pretty well restricted to the three Rs and from which they had no opportunity to qualify for higher education. The main deficiency with this system was that a child from a town where places were more plentiful might gain access with a mark of say seventy percent while a child in another town might miss out with a much better mark. But enough of the social comment.

The exam was treated extremely seriously by teachers and students alike and the atmosphere on exam day was tense as the nervous eleven-year-olds congregated in huddles in the otherwise empty playground, the rest of the school enjoying a day off. At ten to nine, the school doors swung open and we were ushered into specially set up classrooms where stern examiners warned us about cheating, advised us to check the pencils that we'd sharpened and resharpened at least twice and then proceeded to lay very official-looking exam papers, all properly printed on pale blue paper, face down in front of each of us. There they sat, daring us to take a peek, until the railway clock above the blackboard ticked to nine precisely, the examiner checked the

Queen Victoria School in the 1930s.

stopwatch on the desk in front of him, rechecked the clock and told us to go. A silence that was almost palpable fell over us, broken only by the scratching of well chewed pencils, the odd sigh or nervous cough, the harsh and incessant ticking of the clock and the rattle of the local trains as they headed into and out of Shields station at regular intervals.

The exam covered all of the studies we'd completed over the previous six years and the only bit I ever remembered was a section where you had to enter the nationality of the people who lived in various countries, for example, Holland = Dutch, Denmark = Danes etc. One of these stupid questions stuck in my mind throughout the exam and eluded every effort to dislodge it from the tip of my tongue where it stubbornly remained until the final bell rang. Once out, I flew through Scott's Park (not on the grass of course), past the green bus stop, along Saville Street, helter-skelter along the lane and up the outside stairs to Grandma's where she and Ma were waiting for me. I puffed and panted while Wor Ma confirmed that the good people who lived in Switzerland were of course Swiss and I rationalised that if I couldn't get something as simple as that, then I most certainly couldn't have got the harder bits right.

Some months later the whole school was assembled in the main hall to hear the result of our efforts. Mr Sparks swept in, the gown that he wore only on very special occasions flapping in his breeze as he stomped to centre stage where, flanked by his teaching staff, he adjusted his mortar to exactly the correct degree of tilt before surveying us all with that withering all-seeing, all-knowing look that headmasters must practice for hours in front of a mirror in the privacy of their own homes. Satisfied that all was in order, he started off by saying how proud he was to report that the Grading Examination results had exceeded his most optimistic expectations with no less than twelve students passing this toughest of tests. When the applause had died down, he proceeded to read out the individual names, in a style that has since been adopted by a succession of Academy Award hosts. My mate Billy Ray was one of the first to be called, then a kid whose Da owned a bike shop on Saville Street, then two cousins who got an extra cheer, then another seven I don't recall and last but obviously by no means least; Norman Christenson. His twelve disciples ascended the stage where the Head went on some more about what a great bunch we were before giving each of us a firm manly handshake and a plastic protractor which he hinted would guide us through the hard years ahead. I remember thinking at the time that after all the fine words and ringing praises, a clarty plastic half moon was just a wee bit anticlimactic but I suppose it's the thought that counts. When I arrived home, Wor Ma was up to her eyes in the scullery, her sleeves rolled up and her hair hanging in whisps over her steam wet face as she possed yet another load of washing. She cried and cuddled me when I gave her the news and said 'Your Da would have been proud of you.'

While this was obviously one of my happier days at QV, it wasn't *the* happiest, that distinction clearly going to a memorable night a year or so previously when a German airman, looking for the gasworks (because all the old women reckoned every bomb dropped on Britain was really intended for our gas works) missed by a fair bit and instead landed smack on top of the Wesley Church just across the road from QV.

Our joy was unconfined as we turned up the next morning to find our Alma Mater a mess of broken windows with doors blasted off hinges and rubble strewn from one end of the playground to the other. Hopes that this was the end of school for the duration of the war, and who knew but maybe even for ever, were quickly dashed as within days we were crammed into Western School, a rough old sandstone edifice that would have been massively improved by a good bomb blast.

After some weeks among the lower town toughs, our school was sufficiently repaired for us to return and each of us was given something rare and important to carry back. As we wound our way like so many laden ants along Howdon Road and up Coach Lane to our proper nest, I was entrusted with a cardboard box full of those colourful little squares of sticky paper that we were forever using to make maps or pretty patterns. Everything went swimmingly until the very last, just as we neared the charred and blackened remains of the Wesley Church, when a sharp blast of wind whipped over the railway embankment and, despite my panic-stricken efforts, blew the contents of the box all over the road and onto the railway lines as the other kids cheered my feeble efforts to rescue two or three bent and bedraggled squares. And so my illustrious, and at times starring, career at Queen Victoria Primary School came to a mortifying and shameful close.

Everyone I'd ever known had gone to 'Ralphies' (Ralph Gardiner School) and it had never once crossed my mind that I wouldn't be joining them there. I knew the names of most of the teachers, which ones were OK which ones were to be avoided, what lessons you got and I was quite looking forward to joining my cousins and neighbours there. Instead, here I was getting fitted-out in a poncy little cap and a fancy green blazer with the Tynemouth coat of arms proudly emblazoned on the breast pocket and all trimmed with gold braid that Wor Ma would spend the next few years trying to keep reasonably clean.

Instead of the three minute walk along West Percy Road, I was preparing to meet a bunch of snobs and upstarts (because it was a well known fact that only snobs and kids from Tynemouth went to the High School) at a school miles and miles, or at least fifteen minutes walk away from Silkeys Lane.

The council that built Queen Victoria School obviously had some sort of 'two for the price of one' deal going with the designing architect because if buildings had brothers and sisters then QV and the High School obviously belonged to the same family. My new school was a bit bigger and a bit grander and, at three storeys high, just a bit taller, but it was still the same red brick, the same tall windows, the same yellow key stones and the same arched doors and parapets. Like QV, the classes mixed both sexes quite naturally together but for some reason I never could figure out, we had segregated playgrounds where the girls skipped and played netball in theirs while we kicked and batted balls in ours. The inside was certainly more impressive than QV. Our classrooms occupied the outer perimeter of the building, with the main assembly area occupying the centre. Here each morning we'd climb to pre-arranged seats in the high sloping auditorium where we'd look down on Mr Smedley, the Head and the entire staff ringed behind him in their mortars and black gowns. We'd sing a couple of hymns, say our prayers and listen to any important announcements the headmaster might have to make from his posh rostrum before spilling out to our individual classrooms.

The upper floors housed well-equipped science labs and art studios and there were separate outside buildings that catered for the more practical subjects like woodwork and metalwork plus a music room where Mr Wolstenholme played classical records and had us listening for the trill of the piccolo or the deep booming grandeur of the bassoon. I seemed to spend most of these sessions listening for the bell that moved us on to somewhere else. Those first few days were like a series of Christmases all rolled into one. Each afternoon I'd fly down to

Silkeys Lane where an expectant audience waited for me to heft the still stiff and still leathery smelling haversack off my shoulders and onto the front room table.

Wor Ma and the kids crowded around and boggled respectfully as I carefully withdrew a veritable library of brand new text books, some covering old and trusted subjects while others contained mysterious algebraic equations or geometric shapes or even foreign languages. A history textbook was an immediate hit, raising great giggles and much finger pointing when one of the lads found a picture of a Grecian urn decorated with warlike figures whose willies dangled for all to see. Then of course there were all the different exercise books, some with almost a hundred pages, an unheard of amount of paper in a house where the biggest piece of drawing paper was usually the margins around the *Shields Evening News*. We'd eventually learn to nick pages out of the centre of these by carefully prising up the staples that held them in place and just as carefully replacing them but evil thoughts like this were still far away as the five of us stood around turning them over, admiring the Tynemouth coat of arms emblazoned on the covers and heeding Wor Ma's umpteenth warning to 'Watch wor dorty fingers.' So here I was, fully equipped for the start of a life of scholarship and study.

There were a number of subtle and not so subtle reminders that we High Schoolies were just a bit different to the secondary school kids. It wasn't that we sneered or spat at them in the street or anything like that but our hours were marginally different, our uniforms set us apart and of course we had the privilege of doing homework. In retrospect, our homework load was probably much lighter than today's primary kids have to cope with but to someone who looked at school as a strictly nine to four activity, the idea of giving up those treasured after school play hours to sit over cruddy old school books was less than attractive. My very first homework assignment was set by a very plain, dour and ungallic lady who taught French. I'm sure she must have explained pretty carefully what was expected of us, because she explained everything very carefully and at least twice, but as I sat at the kitchen table, the warm evening sun pouring through the window and the yells and screams of the other kids ringing in my ears, her words disappeared and my brain went into fast forward. For the life of me I couldn't see why we had to be bothered with grammar and verbs and nouns and tenses and all of that rubbish for something as simple as French. Flicking to the back of the text book I quickly dashed through the English/French vocabulary, swapped words just like they did when they solved spy codes in the *Wizard* and in ten minutes I was outside kicking a ball with my mates. Strangely, Miss Whatsername was less than impressed when she marked my efforts. She went to great lengths to explain that Tynemouth High School had established its own

Norman in his Tynemouth High School uniform.

teaching methods over many years, that they were extremely happy with these methods and that at this stage they'd be deeply grateful if I'd forget the Christenson Quick Study method and comply with their standard study procedures.

This incident clearly proved two things. Firstly, I was going to have serious problems with Miss Whatsername who obviously hated me and secondly Tynemouth High was going to have just as many problems coping with my undoubted brilliance. Their insistence on hard work and diligence sounded fine within the confines of those hallowed halls but tended to fade when the endless light nights beckoned or in the dark of winter when the latest Biggles adventure had me trapped in my armchair cockpit in front of a roaring fire. Naturally enough, these warm relaxed evenings inevitably led to cold hard mornings when Norman, all remorse and guilt-ridden, found himself crouched in toilets or cloakrooms desperately trying to cadge answers or copy notes to meet some immutable final deadline. The solution to these problems was as smart as the behaviour that created them in the first place. I'd take a few days unofficial leave to catch up. After the truant-catcher returned me to school, Mr Smedley gave me a good talking-to which didn't hurt much plus two sticks across my bum which did and which left two great wheals that I never saw but which were much admired by friends who inspected them in the toilets later.

At the end of second year, students selected the special subjects he or she needed to further their chosen career paths. Would-be teachers took languages, future scientists pressed on with chemistry and physics, doctors and pharmacists laboured through Latin and biology. Those who simply wanted an easy life took art and woodwork. My interest in languages had never quite recovered from that first run in with the French teacher from Hell even though by this stage I was fluent enough to ask for the door to be opened or to enquire after the location of my auntie's pen. Biology wasn't a strong point, my greatest single achievement here being a drawing of an amoeba that looked awfully like one of those islands where X marked the spot where the pirates' treasure was buried. Ditto for chemistry where my only claim to fame stemmed from an unfortunate incident when I accidentally snapped off one of the tall copper water taps, creating a magnificent fountain that soaked everything and everyone within about a ten foot radius. I wasn't too bad at normal maths, like how many twopenny apples for a shilling, and geometry made some sort of sense to me as opposed to the algebraic formulae which made absolutely no sense at all. After all, who the hell cared what the power of x was.

Faced with these academic realities, the choice of art and woodwork was painless and entirely logical although it must be pointed out in my defence that I did have a long standing interest in all things artistic. Our meagre package of family heirlooms contains two or three creased and somewhat tattered posters that won competitions for me when I was at QV. They show nicely coloured-in planes and ships and tanks and soldiers, all bombing or sinking or shooting blokes in long black wellies with funny helmets with swastikas all over them and neatly painted slogans like SAVE FOR THE BRAVE. How I didn't end up in Maddison Avenue with a background like that, still mystifies me.

Woodwork turned out to be the only subject at High School that ever brought me any immediate or tangible advantage. Most homes in those days had at least one cracket, a small wooden stool on which people perched themselves in front of the fire when it was too much trouble to pull up a bigger chair. It just so happened that a cracket was our third project after the chamfered tea pot stand and the pair of chamfered candle sticks that adorned Wor Ma's sideboard for years. The first one I made for Wor Ma was much admired by Mrs Stutt from next door who parted with a whole half crown when I produced a second edition to grace her front room. Orders from Aunts and Uncles quickly followed

TELEPHONE: NORTH SHIELDS 34
STATION - NORTH SHIELDS L.N.E.R.
HEADMASTER:

J. H. Smedley,
B.Sc.(Oxon) M.Sc.(B'ham).

INTERVIEWS : WEDNESDAYS 2-4 P.M.
OTHER TIMES BY APPOINTMENT ONLY.
REF. No.:

JHS/LID.

HIGH SCHOOL,
HAWKEY'S LANE,
NORTH SHIELDS.

May 1948.

NORMAN CHRISTENSON was a pupil in this School
from September 1944 to April 1948 reaching the Fourth Year
of the Main Secondary Course.

He is a quietly attentive worker of very fair
mental ability, cheerful and well behaved. The quality of his
work under manual instruction suggests that he will do well
in the trade he has chosen, carpentry and joinery.

HEADMASTER.

Norman's 'testimonial' from Tynemouth High School.

and my woodworking lessons soon turned into a glorified cracket
assembly line. Old Mr Chadwick who taught us to plane and drill and
bevel and make dovetails and mortice and tenon joints must have
wondered what sort of family needed cracket after cracket after cracket
but if he did, he never raised either of his immensely bushy eyebrows
and consequently I enjoyed brief periods of practical cabinet making
and unexpected wealth.

'Ordinary' kids left school at fourteen but we 'special' High
Schoolies stayed till we were sixteen or, with special permission, at
fifteen which I turned in November 1947. By then I was determined to
put all this academic rubbish behind me and head for the excitement,
the adventure and the massive monetary rewards beckoning from
Smith's Docks. Mr Smedley invited Wor Ma up to school to discuss my
application for early release and he gave both of us a great talking-to
about how pupils were like horses. Some, like brothers Brian and
Derek, were destined to live in cold dark stables and to pull heavy
loads up and down life's bumpy highways. Others, like myself, were
fortunate enough to train in the best of stables, like Tynemouth High
School, they could eventually become magnificent racing
thoroughbreds, like him. I must confess that did seem like a pretty
compelling argument at the time but I couldn't see myself running in
the three thirty at Ascot and so Norman left those hallowed halls for
the last time, condemned for ever to a life of heavy load pulling.

The headmaster, in his final reference described me as being 'a

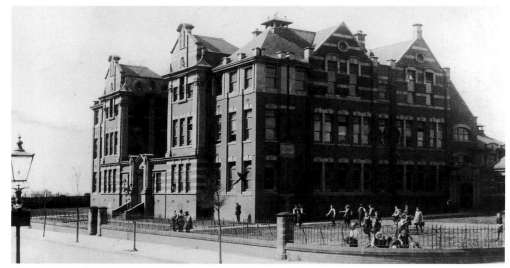

The High School.

quietly attentive worker of very fair mental ability, cheerful and well behaved', he went on to assert that 'the quality of my work under manual instruction suggested that I would do well in my chosen trade of carpentry or joinery.'

When I sat and read these comments later at home I had to look twice to make sure he hadn't given me someone else's documents by mistake. I had just completed four of the longest years of my life during which time this 'quiet and attentive worker' must have been told to 'shut up and get on with his work' at least five times a day. He'd obviously forgotten to take into account the hours spent on detention, just me and a supervising teacher in a quiet and otherwise empty classroom, him marking books and me writing hundreds of lines like 'The answer to who first crossed the Atlantic by air is not Biggles.' The late book in which Billy Ray and I were frequent entries must have gone missing as must the comments of Mr Fanstone who interviewed all latecomers and who reckoned he didn't believe Billy when he claimed he was delayed because his Ma had had a baby. Neither of us at that stage could figure out why he wouldn't believe him just cos he reckoned he'd already used that excuse three times in the past six months.

The old place didn't seem quite so bad as I walked out for the last time but despite the trials and tribulations awaiting me in the hard world outside, I don't ever recall hankering to get back. I do sometimes think if I'd applied myself and done my homework and paid attention, my life might have been so different. I could have been a captain of industry, or a town councillor, or the Member for Tynemouth or even somebody really powerful like the parking attendant who checks all the disabled cars that fill Bedford Street. Just as well we never know, isn't it?

BOYHOOD DAYS

Norman and dog at Silkeys Lane fields with the 'famous' static water tank.

Our formative years weren't all spent doing times tables and being belted around the head by fossilised teachers. A master at the High School once told us that the rest of the world had a climate but we only had weather. Despite this somewhat negative opinion of our magnificent Northern climate, we managed to spend almost all of our leisure times out of doors, playing and exploring and generally managing to keep ourselves amused. No doubt our parents, stuck in small houses with a bunch of noisy and rambunctious kids, went out of their way to encourage these outdoor activities although to the best of my recollection, we didn't need much prodding to get into the great outdoors. The front street was our primary playground. Traffic-free, apart from the odd passing workman on his bike, the milkman or coalman's horse and cart or the weekly visit by the Rington's Tea man. This was our very own strip of concrete where we kicked and chalked and ran and played the games that seemed to have their own season proscribed on some mysterious but nevertheless real calendar.

An advert for Rington's Tea.

The tops that had all of us whipping madly one week, were replaced by metal hoops that we guided for miles until they in turn gave way to home-made kites or tin can stilts or whatever the next craze might be. The long summer nights were filled with team games that used up some of the pent-up energy built up during long days spent being seen but not heard on hard school seats. Games like cut-a-bay and tin-a-block and jack-jack-your biscuits are burning were particularly popular. This was probably because any number could play, no equipment was needed and you made the rules up as you went along. Add to that, the fact that nobody won or lost and their attractiveness becomes even more apparent. There were more traditional contests like hide and seek and leapfrog, all of which were strictly segregated except when you got a few of the girls interested in a game of 'catchy kissy' but this was usually a bit of a let down as the girls you fancied wouldn't be caught and it was almost impossible to shake off the ones you hated.

The girls monopolised the pavement with their chalked 'bays' into which they slid stones and hopped and skipped and danced over the numbered squares in a cissy sort of ritual that we lads would never have been seen dead doing. Skipping was another predominantly female activity. Two swung the long heavy rope, nicked from one of the local shipyards, as the rest tucked their skirts into their grey bloomers and darted under the swinging rope as the rest recited, 'Raspberry, Strawberry, Marmalade, Jam, tell me the name of your young man.' We lads sneered at such girly activities though secretly we were dying to have a go.

These popular games got the push from time to time as we relived last Saturday's matinee from the Howard. Bays and balls were temporarily set aside as we galloped around, smacking our bums with one hand and discharging our index finger six shooter with the other in a way that Gene Autrey could never have envisaged. The recipients of the bullets were invariably the 'Red Indians' who hung a bedraggled feather from one of Mrs Wright's chickens behind one ear while making appropriate noises by whooping and waggling a finger in their mouth all at the same time. Errol Flynn was far and away our number one hero and Gladstone's hardware shop did a roaring trade as every other kid in Shields queued up to get their hands on the bamboo garden stakes that quickly became trusty longbows that could throw bamboo arrows anywhere up to five feet while our parents ranted and raved and swore we'd put somebody's eye out.

Swimming was popular during the summer although why anyone would consider entering those freezing cold waters is something that I now find incomprehensible. At the start of each season, we'd nag Wor Ma unmercifully till she came up with the one and six that bought a season ticket to Hawkeys Lane pool, a red bricked utilitarian establishment that didn't look much from outside and in fact looked little better from within. Just about every day saw us charging past the 'Ticket Man's' little window, waving the season tickets that would soon be so tattered and torn we'd need to paste them to bits of cardboard. Clothes were dragged off, quickly wrapped in towels and deposited on the long green form that ran the length of the top tier as we hopped back down the steps in our hand-knitted swimmers that looked great till they actually got wet and the crutch hung like a sodden woollen udder between your legs. All of us took our first strokes here in the hooped arrangement that the instructors used to drag us up and down the length of the pool till we were blinded by the chlorine and our lungs filled to capacity with pool water. Despite these advanced training techniques, all of us learned to swim after a fashion and we'd run home to Wor Ma, all crinkled blue fingers and runny noses, to tell her how many laps we'd done today.

The Romans had their chariots, the Chinese their rickshaws, the Eskimos their sledges but we had the conveyance to beat all conveyances in the shape of the most illustrious Geordie racing bogie. In its simplest form, the common or garden bogie consisted of a short plank onto which two sets of second hand pram wheels had been attached at either end, the back ones fixed while the front pair swivelled to provide a rough and ready steering mechanism. The driver manoeuvred the contraption by resting his feet on either side of the front axle or by frantically pulling on a set of reins attached thereabouts. The usually mangled wheels, allied with this somewhat unsophisticated guidance system left a lot to be desired insofar as precision handling was concerned and the very best of bogies usually behaved in an entirely contrary and unpredictable manner that has only since been reproduced in the shape of today's supermarket trolley. Braking was even more primitive and was performed in one of three ways. The first involved jamming the soles of both feet onto the front wheels to provide a reasonably gradual deceleration. The second (and considerably more painful) method involved the insertion of one foot into the rapidly spinning spokes. The third and more practical method consisted of simply crashing into whichever wall, tree or gutter happened to be most conveniently situated in front of the conveyance when it had reached its most terrifying top speed which was often faster than a brisk walk. Most bogies tended to have relatively short life spans and we spent many more hours building or repairing them than we ever did actually riding them.

We did, from time to time, get involved in more organised activities like the YMCA or Boys Clubs where sadistic instructors made men out of us by hitting us in the face with boxing gloves. These memberships tended to lapse fairly quickly. Cubs and Scouts were also popular and, like so many others, I could fasten a woggle and Dib Dib Dib with the best of them. The other kids learned to tie sheep shanks and slip knots and clovehitches while I turned bits of rope into knots that they hadn't thought up names for yet. We also had a scouting book that was full of helpful hints like:

> More blankets below Johnny was told
> But Johnny knew better so Johnny caught cold.

It also contained page upon page of the badges that were awarded for proficiency in a million and one things. Some of the older kids had armfuls of these that they wore with all the smugness of someone who knows something you don't. I went for weeks, and they still hadn't given me a badge so I never went back.

Every Christmas saw one or the other of us get some sort of indoor game that proved the truth of the old saying that 'The Family That Plays Together, Fights Together.' These usually got stashed away for the inevitable rainy day but just as inevitably when we were driven to drag them out we'd find the dice was missing from the Snakes and Ladders or half the draughts pieces had gone the journey or we'd misplaced the bit that tiddled your wink. Blow football was always a hit until somebody stood on the table tennis ball or till the ends of the blow pipes became so soggy that even we wouldn't put them in our mouths. Brother Brian once scored a memorable 'Goal of the Week' when he blew so hard that a loose front tooth flew out the pipe and ricochet off the ball. This was disallowed on a technicality so we all ended up

Boys exercising at Queen Victoria School.

fighting as we inevitably did before heading outside to play proper games. Like climbing trees, digging holes, throwing stones, forming gangs, making camps, riding bikes, catching crabs, kicking tins, playing chucks, whipping tops, flying kites, building dams, lashing hoops, hunting newts, collecting tadpoles, chasing girls or just sitting around moaning about how bored we were and how there was never anything to do around this place.

A family home in North Shields in the 1930s. Homes like this were soon to be demolished as families, like the Christenson's, moved to the new Ridges Estate.

THE WAR

A Union Jack still flies in bomb-damaged Cartington Road.

As adults it's hard to think of anything worse than a war. For our parents and grandparents, the prospect of a second conflict only twenty one years after the first one had taken its dreadful toll, must have been overwhelming. To us kids however, the war was firstly a great adventure as we went through the elaborate preparations and then simply a part of our lives that was as normal as getting out of bed or going to school. I was just a couple of months away from my seventh birthday when Mr Chamberlain made the historic announcement that everybody in England must have been listening to. Wor Ma reckons I broke into tears, probably at the sight of all the sad faces around me but I don't recollect that, I do remember marching through the streets with the other neighbouring kids singing a song that went something like:

> Vote vote vote for Winston Churchill
> Churchill's sure to win the war
> Cos he'll make the Germans run
> And he'll kick them up the bum
> And we'll never see the Germans any more.

This show of strength must have filled the enemy with considerable fear and trepidation because nothing even remotely warlike happened for a considerable time afterwards, and I'm sure we kids were convinced that the war was going to be like all the other things the adults told us we'd get to see 'when we were twenty-one'. Despite the lack of action, there were plenty of changes going on all around us as preparations were made for what wiser heads realised was bound to follow.

Our beloved beaches were locked away behind miles of tangled and rapidly rusting barbed wire while hastily erected pill boxes and gun emplacements sprouted like concrete mushrooms on hillocks and cliff tops. An artillery regiment moved into the ancient Tynemouth Priory and we'd gawp at the bloke in the sentry box and watch from the cliff tops as they drilled behind their guns that pointed expectantly over the gap between the piers. Signposts were uprooted and removed so that spies wouldn't know where they were going while a band of white overalled workmen went round the town obliterating any signs that might give them a clue where they were. The Tyne Laundry, after a few well aimed brush strokes, became The —— Laundry, the *Shields Evening News* was just your common or garden *Evening News* and businesses like Tyne and Tees Traders, basically became nameless. These actions had little or no effect on the locals who knew every inch of the town off by heart but they would undoubtedly have had a profoundly destabilising effect on any Germans who hadn't thought to buy a map before the war started.

I always had this picture, in my mind's eye, of a regiment of Huns, all steel helmets and field grey uniforms, marching along Saville Street and stopping the first little cloth-capped Geordie they chanced upon.

'Excuse me schweinehund (because in the war pictures, they always called everybody that before they smacked them in the gob with their riding crop). Is dis der Nord Shields gertownshippe?'

'Whey no man,' the little Geordie would reply, keeping a dead straight face. 'This is bliddy Henley on Thames.'

'Ach Schiddt,' the officer would explode, furiously screwing his monocle back into place, 'Back to der boat mein mennen' and they'd all goose step their way back along Saville Street and England would be saved to go on and beat them in the World Cup at a later date.

But it wasn't only the armed forces that were making all the preparations. Housewives sat at home and filled little packets of pepper to throw in the eyes of German paratroops, Home Guards jumped all over our back field wielding broom handles as make-believe rifles and we all got fitted-out with our gas masks. Surprisingly there was quite a wide selection of these. Soldiers had the proper ones with the goggly eyes and the breathing tube that led into a haversacked cartridge carried on their chests. The masks that mothers and we bigger kids had, were self-contained units with straps that your parents adjusted so tight that you would have died trying to get it on if there'd ever been a real gas attack. They stank of rubber and stuck to your face like glue but made terrific farting noises if you lifted one side off your cheek and blew hard. Masks for small kids were similar but came in colours like red and blue and had a little nose flap that waggled up and down as

A young 'un tries out a gas mask.

they breathed in and out. The idea was that this would amuse the little 'uns and take their minds off the fact that they were wearing a gas mask but I'm not sure if they could even see the waggly nose through their eye pieces so maybe everybody else should have had the funny nose. A bloke arrived one day with a big cardboard box containing the special one that we needed for baby Doreen. She was supposed to fit completely inside this black rubber pod that had a perspex window like a small TV screen, through which you could check what shade of blue the baby was, while operating a concertina-like pump that provided the necessary air supply. I'm not sure how old Doreen was at the time but she was obviously old enough to have made up her mind that nothing on God's earth was going to get her inside that rubbery prison. Kicking and struggling and alternately stiffening and flopping around like a rag doll, she screamed and howled as Wor Ma sweated and swore and wrestled to get her inside the life-saving apparatus. It finally dawned on all of us that there was no way we were ever going to get her into that mask and so the red faced and redder eyed Doreen was reprieved and the mask disappeared into the darkest recesses of the cupboard under the stairs where it collected dust for the next five years. The rest of us were condemned to carry ours, like an albatross around out necks, the cardboard carry-cases becoming increasingly battered and bent as they banged against hip and thigh and on every wall or railing that we passed on our daily trips to and from school.

Protected against the gas that never came, our town fathers set about providing us with the shelters that would protect us from the bombs which certainly did. Folk in the older and more built-up parts of town had to rely on their own, or neighbours, cellars or on the triple brick and concrete above ground shelters like the one on the spare ground behind Uncle Tom's Cabin that Grandma Mac used. The people at the top end of Silkeys Lane had a big underground shelter that provided us with endless hours of spectating. The first team of workmen laboured away to dig a huge square hole that might have taken a couple of days with modern earth-moving equipment but took considerably longer, relying as they did, on nothing more advanced than picks and shovels and the sweat of their collective brows. They were closely followed by teams of concreters and bricklayers who rapidly built the four-sided passageway that was concreted over and buried with the soil removed in the first place. Dank and airless and perpetually cold and dark, this shelter was entered via a concrete ramp that gave easy access but also collected all the rain in a perpetual puddle at the bottom so that wellies were compulsory footwear. Inhospitable and uncomfortable as these were, they still gave protection to those who didn't have a cellar or shelter of their own. They also provided a not so cosy nook for courting couples who didn't have anywhere better to go and some of our first wartime casualties were the young lasses who popped in there for a bit of a cuddle and came out with a bit of a problem.

When they'd finished this shelter, the workmen moved across West Percy Road to the top of our front field where they set about building our very own Static Water Tank to hold emergency supplies for fire-fighting purposes. The guy who decided to build these must have been the world's greatest pessimist as the one thing we were never short of, war or no war, was rain. I would have thought that any water tank about thirty by twenty feet in size and built from best quality British bricks would have been, by definition, pretty static but maybe they meant stagnant which is what it rapidly became. After any sort of dry spell, which in Shields meant anything more than three days without pouring rain, the pool assumed a green algael appearance that would have had earth scientists converging on it in their hundreds today. And it had an odour all its own, due no doubt to the collection of old mattresses, assorted items of used-clothing and occasional dead cat that floated on its murky surface. However, neither this nor the strands of barbed wire which guarded its three feet high walls, presented any sort of a deterrent to us as we leaned over the side to launch the paper boats that we bombarded with stones and rocks. We had a local dog called Pilot which nobody owned but which followed us around just happy to yap at our heels and chase anything we'd throw for it. It developed this amazing trick of running at the water tank, leaping onto the wall and somehow avoiding the barbed wire as it dived headlong into the water before bounding back out and covering us in stinking spray as we tried to escape. That dog was the only thing in Shields that smelled worse than the water tank.

The Christenson family preparations climaxed the day the council truck came and dumped the components for our very own Anderson Shelter in our front garden. We had a great time rocking in the curved corrugated sections that would eventually encase us before checking out the lengths of angle iron and the hessian bag of heavy nuts and bolts that would fasten everything together. Dad originally planned to plant ours in the back yard and after much measuring with string lines and stakes, he set about the task of digging the three or four feet deep hole in which the shelter would be assembled. Sleeves rolled up and stripped off to his waistcoat, he picked and shovelled and shovelled and picked his way through a long summer afternoon and evening as we 'helped' and encouraged and the hole grew steadily deeper and deeper. Rushing out the next morning, anxious to get on with the project, we found Dad's hard dug hole to now be three parts filled with water that must have seeped in from some subterranean stream. Muttering a few well-chosen words, he set about returning the soil and clarts from whence they came and it speaks volumes for his shovelling ability that he managed to complete this task before any one of us slid into its murky depths.

He had more luck in the front garden where we soon had a beautifully dry square hole smack in the centre of what we euphemistically called the front lawn, a pretty barren little collection of assorted weeds, a few straggly bits of privet and a garden bed in which nothing ever grew despite Dad's best horticultural efforts. The six curved sections were jockeyed into position and bolted together, the bits for either end set in place and in what seemed like no time at all, our shelter stood all grey and galvanised in its tailor made excavation.

Dad – Herbert Christenson.

All that remained was for Dad to bury his creation under the spoil from the hole and it was almost ready for occupation. Ready perhaps but not, at this stage, overly comfortable with its coldly sweating metal walls and muddy clay floor. But great plans were afoot and over the ensuing weeks, he installed a planked floor that was softened by the addition of an old clippy mat. Two low forms were set along either long wall and a pair of bunks, complete with thin flock mattresses sat snugly across the end furthest away from the entrance. A neat wooden door was fitted into the small entrance and draped with a piece of tarpaulin that kept the wind and rain out and finally a kerosene lamp was hung in the centre where it provided a weak smoky light and crowned anyone over four feet who was foolish enough to move around the interior.

Some weeks later Dad arrived home proudly pushing a barrow on which nestled a smallish cast iron stove. Soil was reshovelled off the roof, the stove was manoeuvred through the door and connected to the smoke stack that stuck up through the hole that Dad had cut in the corrugated iron and we all stood back speechless and lost in wonderment at the thought that ordinary folk could have it this good. Leaving us to sit and admire his handiwork, Dad bustled off, returning shortly with a bucket of coal, some bits of firewood, and a scrunched up *Shields Evening News* all of which soon disappeared into the nifty little cast iron door on the front of the stove. Striking a match, he lit a well-earned Woodbine before applying the flame to the fire. Drawing back a great lungful of smoke, he sat back on the form with us, to bask in the warmth of the fire and the growing admiration of his family. The paper soon flared into life, and we could hear the sticks crackling away as they too took hold. Sadly we couldn't observe much else of what was happening as the stove started to emit small puffs of white smoke, then slightly bigger puffs of grey smoke and then great clouds of smoke that had us all scrambling through the door and back into the garden where we wiped our eyes and wondered why not even one little wisp was emerging from the stack that was designed for that specific purpose. Dad re-entered the shelter when the worst of the fug had dissipated and raked out the unburned coals, and poked things up the chimney, checked fastenings and shook the stack and tried again with exactly the same result. Every now and then when the mood took him, he'd return to his nemesis, determined to fix whatever ailed it but all to no avail and it spent the rest of the war cold and sullen and useless, a permanent reminder of how cosy our frozen extremities might have been.

Dad must have wondered if all his efforts had been just so much wasted time as life went on pretty well as before. We all practised our air raid drills and learned the difference between the ululating warning siren and the long drawn-out all clear, but through all of this the shelter sat cold and unused. Elsewhere, even more preparations went on apace especially along the riverbanks where the skies were gradually filling with the big silver barrage balloons that ducked and floated over our heads like so many ungainly fat space ships. The theory was that they were placed strategically so that low flying enemy planes had to weave their way between them and the earth below. In actual fact, they never attained any great altitude and I don't know if any daring Red Baron with a patch over his eye was ever daft enough not to fly over the top of them. They did, however, provide great entertainment and the silvery grey plastic material was much sought after to make tablecloths, weatherproof pram covers and even once, it was rumoured, a wedding dress! Our nearest balloon site was on a spare block of ground just opposite the ferry landing and we'd stand for ages watching the mixed crew of soldiers and soldierettes get their charge airborne. The partially filled balloon flopped and rolled around like a recently landed whale, all lumps and wrinkles as the generator roared and puffed blue smoke into the crowd and the required mixture of gas and air into the tethered monster. As it's interior filled and swelled, it started to take on a life of its own, bobbing and rolling and tugging at the sandbag weighted lines that fought to keep it grounded until it was fully inflated. This was the bit we liked best. WRACs and soldiers screamed orders at each other, grabbed lines, loosened sandbags and, in the process, got dragged all around the spare lot. Through puddles and patches of nettles, into adjoining walls, digging in heels, scrambling to get off the seat of their pants, loosening some ropes and hanging on to others for dear life as the great grey monster seemed to take on a mind of its own. Finally, to the accompaniment of a confused and almost hysterical chorus of screamed commands, all hands released their ropes and flew to the perimeter of the block as the balloon ducked and bobbed like a drunken dinosaur before slowly but surely rising into the air as a soldier on the truck operated the winch that let out yard after yard of retaining rope. We kids cheered and waved, the older spectators smiled proudly and the soldiers sat against the truck and lit up their Woodbines. I don't know how often the balloons went up and down or what the soldiers did when they were just bobbing away over the Tyne but I'm sure the Army found something to keep them occupied.

Most of these preparations had gone on during the long summer nights when the blackout was something none of us had had to come to grips with. This all changed as the days shortened and we had to develop the navigational skills that would get us around on pitch black nights when you literally couldn't see your hand in front of your face. By now, every window had been painted black or was draped in the blackout curtains that hung inside your normal decorative ones. Older folk, like Grandma, had little torches to guide them over kerbs and up and down stairs and to help them avoid the lamp posts that caught many an unwary pedestrian. Luckily there were few cars to start with fewer still as petrol became scarcer and the streets were left to the odd bus that managed to find its way around with slitted headlights and blinds drawn over the dimly-lit interior, the conductor reeling off the stops as they continued to do long after hostilities ceased.

The dark and the blackout created our very own breed of mini-Hitlers in the form of the local Air Raid Wardens, a bunch of whizzened old grandads and retired parkies who leapt at the chance to escape their wives for a few hours and to boss everybody else around. All dolled up in dark greatcoats, made official with the addition of an AIR RAID WARDEN armband, they'd don their tin helmets, sling their gas masks, hang their referee's whistle around their scrawny necks and stomp forth into the night.

Eagle-eyed, and absolutely single-minded, their vocabulary consisted of four words and four words only, 'PUT THAT LIGHT OUT' which they'd scream at any poor soul who inadvertently let even the faintest gleam escape as they answered the front door or sneaked out the back to go to the toilet. We used to love to wander the darkened streets, put on our deepest voices and yell those dreaded words through the letter box of any poor old soul who was too daft or too deaf to pick out our high-pitched voices. Panic stricken, they'd rush to check curtains that they'd already checked ten minutes ago, convinced that they were directly responsible for guiding the armada of German bombers that was heading straight for them at that very minute.

Granda (standing) was an air raid warden for much of the war.

So now the beaches were mined and barbed wired, the signposts were gone, we had our gas masks, our shelters, our ration cards, the balloons were up and the lights were off. We were ready! Well, almost ready. The final precaution was firmly set in place when we proudly displayed our metal sign in the front window, where all could see the message spelled out in red letters on the stark white background – SP HERE.

This sign indicated to all who passed the Christenson residence that we were the proud guardians of that most important piece of fire-fighting equipment; namely the Stirrup Pump. Looking for all the world like one of those inflators you see people using to pump up car tyres in old movies, it did in fact work in much the same way. One end was plonked in a bucket of water, one foot kept it firmly in place, the handle was pumped furiously up and down and 'voila', a steady stream of water jetted from the end of the short hose. We kids had terrific games with it in the hot weather and a lot of old blokes found they were terrific for watering those spots in the garden that you couldn't get to with the tin cans with nail holes in the bottom. You needed all the dexterity of a one man band to operate it on your own and it was probably easier just to chuck the bucket of water on the fire but that would have been cheating and our status, as the sole guardians of the lower end of Silkeys Lane sole fire fighting implement, no doubt went up more than a few notches the day that sign went in the window.

A stirrup pump in action.

So now, like the Boy Scouts, we really were prepared, and not a moment too soon either. By the time we got into 1940 and '41, the air raid alarms were howling in earnest and with ever-increasing frequency. Many of the early raids didn't amount to much and Dad used to stand just outside the door of the shelter, keeping an eye on proceedings despite Wor Ma's oft stated claim that she didn't care if he got his bliddy head blown off. He dragged me outside one night and sat me on his shoulders to watch a German plane twisting and turning like a falling leaf as it fell smoking to earth caught in a web of searchlights that carefully illuminated its last rites. Wor Ma, like a regular mother hen, didn't look on any of this as a spectator sport and the first notes of the alarm had hardly hit the night air before she was into our bedroom, Doreen under one arm and a bundle of coats and blankets under the other as she yanked and dragged and pushed and chivvied us out of our warm bed and into the cold, cold shelter where we'd be sat shivering and half asleep before the final note died down. Rugs and blankets could then be distributed but despite these, we always seemed to be cold and damp.

As the frequency and intensity of the raids increased, so did the population of our shelter. No matter how quickly we were inside, poor old Mrs Saint who lived at number sixty two was always there first. All wrapped up in a heavy top coat that was almost as long as the nightie underneath, she'd be crouched on her spot on the wooden form, her curlered white hair bobbing in and out of the bucket that she retched and 'Oh my God'd' into for the duration of the raid. Her lodger, old Jack refused to leave his bed no matter how heavy or how close the bombing came and despite the constant claims that 'the silly old bugger would end up spoiling everybody's night by being killed.' He went on to die peacefully therein without ever losing a night's sleep. The Stutts who lived above her made up the balance of our complement. Mr Stutt was a skilled tradesman at Smith's Docks so he was one of the few men around and he used to stand with Dad comparing notes, before Dad took ill late in 1941. So most air raid nights saw Mrs Saint (and her bucket) sharing one form with Mrs Stutt and her three, Wor Ma cuddled the bairn on the other while we three lads either sat alongside her or curled up on one of the perpetually damp bunks.

All of us very quickly became air raid experts. Even the youngest of us, after a relatively short time, could confidently pick the difference between the drumming roar of our own planes, and the deep thrum thrum thrum of the German's. We could also differentiate between artillery fire and bombing, and, as we became even more expert, we could tell fairly accurately whether the descending whistle indicated a comfortably distant bomb blast, a reasonably close one or one that had us with our heads between our legs waiting for imminent explosion. Being imbued with the usual childlike faith in our own immortality, even the closest of close calls was treated as nothing more than yet another adventure to regale our mates with on the morrow.

But if the bombs didn't worry us, the time certainly did. Our concern in this regard stemmed from the fact that we got the following morning off school if the all clear sounded after midnight. And so our parents, who may have been slightly distracted by the bombs dropping all around them, were driven out even closer to distraction by our constant enquiries about what time it was. Only posh people like those in Tynemouth owned proper wrist watches but one of the women invariably grabbed the family alarm clock on their exit from the house and this was continuously checked until either the all clear went to our groans at five to or to our collective sighs at five past midnight.

When we did have a late night and the resultant morning off, we'd be out on the streets bright and early in the quest for shrapnel. Every kid had a box or bag in which they stored their treasured collection of the twisted metal pieces that could be heard clunking onto tiles and roadways at the height of the raids. These would be endlessly examined and appraised and swapped and bartered like so many of the other totally useless things we saved and treasured. A set of tail fins off a German incendiary bomb was the pride of my not inconsiderable collection. This fell through the roof of the Stutt's house one night and only the prompt action of Mr Stutt, who quelled it under the contents of a strategically placed sand bag, restricted the damage to a hole burned in the middle of a rug. I'm not sure how I came to possess this prize ahead of the three Stutt's kids but I probably swapped it for some hardly-used chewing gum or a reasonable sized apple gowk. Many houses did of course come to a more fiery or explosive end than the Stutt's place and these provided a whole new array of playgrounds. Boring old parks with their swings and roundabouts were no match for the bomb sites that abounded. Half demolished staircases still clinging precariously to garishly wallpapered walls became our Mount Everest as we clambered up them, ignoring the bits and pieces of mortar-covered brick that disintegrated around us. Piles of rubble quickly became forts or gun emplacements from which we sallied forth rat tat tatting at the 'Nazis' occupying the cream and green remains of a kitchen where some wife recently tried to turn four ounces of lap into a tasty meal for six. More exotic ruins like the rat-infested old warehouses down Borough Bank or the ruined church opposite gave us a veritable wonderland of creaking rafters, fallen floors, gaping roofs and sagging doors were all the more attractive because they were so strictly forbidden. It never dawned on us that a lot of poor souls had been uprooted and sometimes killed to provide our amusement areas but we were only kids making the most of what was to us a normal state of affairs.

Although it was mainly the older parts of Shields that bore the brunt of the air raids, we had our own near misses in The Ridges, no doubt as the German High Command tried once more to get the nearby gas

The aftermath of bombing at Preston Hospital.

works. A fair bit of Chirton disappeared on one memorable night when a parachute-born mine set off an explosion that rocked us in our shelter over half a mile away. The target of this attack was obviously The Rex cinema where Wor Ma subsequently spent the best years of her life waiting for that last elusive Bingo number. Sat in our shelter one night not long after this earth-shaking incident, we soon realised that tonight's raid was to be one of the heaviest we'd experienced. Through a slight crack in the tarpaulin door cover, we could see reflected in our front room window, the harsh white light from the search lights that criss-crossed the sky, interspersed with flashes as bombs struck and the flickering red of the ensuing flames. The bombers seemed to drone on and on and on, harried always by the anti-aircraft guns that kept up a furious clatter and sent a veritable rainstorm of shrapnel clattering all around. Amid all this background din, we were suddenly aware that the next whistling bomb was much closer than any of the preceding lot and, more importantly, was getting closer by the second. Mr Stutt who'd been giving a running commentary from the door must have arrived at the same conclusion as he started frantically tugging at the

Soldiers clear up in Biddlestone Crescent.

tarpaulin to get inside. The bomb beat him by about half a second. An almighty explosion shook the shelter as though it were in the grip of a major earthquake, the women screamed, the sound of shattering glass was everywhere, Derek flew out of the top bunk and Mr Stutt arrived in a tangle of arms and legs and dust and cordite fumes. Deafened by the noise it seemed at first as if someone had turned off the volume control until slowly, the sounds of the now diminishing raid and a relative silence returned.

We emerged after the all clear to survey the damage. The offending bomb had landed on the pavement on the other side of Silkeys Lane, leaving a fair sized crater and an electric lamp post that leaned over it as if it were inspecting the damage. The front of our block had taken the full force of the explosion that had shattered every pane of glass, sending lethal shards through the lacerated blackout curtains that flapped in tatters around the jagged window frames. Inside, the scene was even worse. Crunching our way over the layer of broken glass, we shielded candles to check a sight that must have been heartbreaking to someone as house proud as Wor Ma. The battered interior was covered in a fine layer of soot dislodged from the chimney by the blast. Everywhere we walked and everything we touched was coated with a mixture of glass particles and soot and left that acrid coaly smell that stayed on long after every nook and cranny had been scrubbed and mopped back to some semblance of order. Council men came the next day and filled in the bomb hole and pushed the lamp post back straight, others worked with panes of glass and putty to restore our windows and those of our neighbours, others fixed loose roof tiles and in a relatively short time our street had returned to normal or as normal as you can get when people are dropping bombs on you.

The German High Command made one more attempt to get either us or the gas works. With the last experience still fresh in our minds, we cringed as the descending bombs whistled closer and closer and closer until their banshee wail seemed they were almost on top of us. Bracing ourselves for the inevitable we crouched in the approved fashion, heads between our legs and hands squashing our ears to our heads as we braced for the shock and explosion that never came. What we got instead was a series of crumping thumps that were felt rather than heard. The mystery was solved early the next morning when a tin hatted policeman rat tatted on our door and explained that we would have to be evacuated until a squad of soldiers disarmed the bombs that had fallen all around us but failed to explode. So much for the famous German super efficiency! Our faces lit up at these glad tidings. We were off to the country where we'd ride horses, chase sheep, climb haystacks and sleep in great soft eiderdowned beds and have eggs every day plus our own Ma to look after us. Unfortunately this wasn't quite the sort of evacuation they had in mind as we soon discovered when Ma dragged us and a few belongings two streets away to Uncle Tom's in Laburnum Avenue where we somehow squeezed into an already crowded house for the few days it took the army to remove the bombs. This episode brought about our sole family casualty when Whiskers, one of our innumerable family cats, disappeared during the upheaval, never to return. It also created some brand new playgrounds in the shape of a few additional craters to the already pockmarked surface of the front field which was rapidly taking on a distinctly lunar appearance. The bottom of these holes invariably held a foot or two of muddy water that made great miniature skating rinks in the winter although the ice wasn't always as thick as we were with the result that we often returned home cold and wet and smelling even worse than Pilot the wonder dog.

The raids gradually subsided after this last intensive campaign and the nightly alarms became things of the past as the town set about clearing up the debris and returning to some sort of normality. While Shields never had to endure the massive raids that other major cities suffered from, we still had more than our fair share of damage, traumas and tragedies. The worst of these, by far, was the Wilkinson's disaster. Wilkinson's bottled soft drinks in their factory in the older east end of town and one of the large cellars beneath the factory, acted as a shelter for many of the people who occupied the adjacent houses. It received a direct hit during one of the heavier raids and the neighbourhood was decimated, and the entire town left mourning, as whole families died in the resulting carnage.

But the war wasn't all about bombs and bravery. It was also a time of shortages with just about everything rationed or unobtainable or both. And whatever was available was always at the end of a queue. Half a pound of sugar, a few ounces of margarine, a couple of eggs and a rasher of bacon sounds today like the makings of an afternoon snack rather than a full week's entitlement but somehow people scraped by. Add to this a minute quantity of red meat, and small dollops of luxuries like tea and jam and biscuits and it makes you wonder how the mums kept their families fed.

As the eldest of the family, one of my responsibilities was to help Wor Ma with the shopping, something I loathed then but only hate today. There used to be this sort of jungle telegraph that quietly but efficiently passed the word around about what was going where. Neighbours or friends stopped each other on the streets or tapped on your door to whisper, in case German spies or them buggers next door overheard, that Barry Nobles' had new potatoes or that Mrs Whatsername around the corner swore blind she'd seen a woman come out of Wilkinson's the butcher with a packet of sausages under her arm. Most of these, no doubt well intentioned, rumours turned out to be just that but every now and again the information was spot on and

A ration book from after the war.

you'd find yourself smugly near the front of a queue that now stretched out of the shop door and half way up the pavement outside. Some old ladies simply tacked themselves onto the end of queues even though they had little idea what awaited them at the other end. They reasoned that it gave them somewhere to stand out of the rain and to have a nice chat with someone you might otherwise never have met plus the added bonus of something they might even want when you got to the counter. A sort of wartime magical mystery tour.

The bane of my life was an old produce type warehouse just around the corner from Northumberland Square. This battered old establishment somehow managed to get more than its fair share of the local potato crop and as a consequence I spent the best part if my formative years outside its sagging double doors in what was undoubtedly the most permanent and slowest moving queue in Shields. Each customer was allotted a set amount, usually half a stone, of the unrationed but scarce spuds and logic suggests that the proprietors might have employed some of the local elves to weigh and pack the required seven pounds of taties into paper bags. But logic didn't have a lot to do with it whereas tradition did. And the long-established tradition was that we all stood in that wet and draughty street while they did it exactly the same way their Granda had done it because if it's good enough for me Granda it's good enough for me. So a little old man in a cap and a long leather apron weighed each lot individually, wiped his nose with the back of his mittened hand, worked out the cost on a piece of paper although each lot was within a halfpenny of the lot before and the lot to come, took your money, gave you change from his leather bag, wiped his nose again and went into the same routine again and again and yet again. The most terrifying part of this experience was the nagging doubt, as you got closer and closer to the door, that you'd be the one who was stood behind the wife who got the last half stone.

Not all shopping expeditions were rewarded with something as exciting as a half stone of unwashed spuds. More exotic products were almost unprocurable as I found out when Dad was in the last days of his illness and I was entrusted with two whole shillings and the responsibility of finding a chemist who still had a bottle of Lucosade on his shelves. Till then, I'd never realised just how many chemists we had and how widespread they were as I tramped from one end of the town to the other, sometimes returning foot-sore and empty-handed but other times marching in triumphantly like Sir Galahad would have done if he'd ever got to take the Holy Grail home to his Ma.

Christmas presented a particular challenge to people like Wor Ma who didn't have much money in the first place and little to spend it on in the second. Certainly, the season wasn't the mega money extravaganza it's turned into since but we kids still got more and more excited as December ticked over and we sent increasingly urgent messages floating up the chimney. Each of us looked forward to whatever we'd set our minds on that year, a couple of books or game for us or a doll or a pram for Doreen. If it was a particularly good year, we might even have got something extra special like a much sought after Meccano set. The boxes always had this picture on the front of a kid of about six, all bright eyed and rosy cheeked, sat with a little spanner in his hand next to this magnificent scale version of the Tower Bridge. On opening the box, you'd find a few tiny nuts and bolts that got lost before Boxing Day and a few bits and pieces that never turned into anything recognisable. I think we must have always got the wrong kit. Putting these minor disappointments to one side, the greatest excitement stemmed from fossicking through our long grey woollen stockings that had on the previous night, been 'hung by the chimney with care'. There was usually a rare apple, sometimes an even rarer orange, a handful of monkey nuts a bar of chocolate and always one of those cellophane wrapped blocks of dates. The nut shells soon covered the front room floor, the apples and oranges disappeared shortly afterwards and the corner of the dates got slightly chewed before being set aside to collect dust and cat hair before Wor Ma eventually threw them out. Each of us hid our chocolate in a top secret hidey hole from whence it could be retrieved and savoured a bit at a time whenever the mood took us. Strangely, no matter how well the rest of us concealed our chocolate treasures, or how carefully we guarded them, they always seemed to vanish whereas Derek's remained intact even though he was forever eating or sucking something sweet. That was what we called the wonder of Christmas.

Men in bowler hats in far off London seemed always to be preoccupied with 'keeping up moral' even though ours never seemed to be all that down. One of their greatest schemes was the 'Holidays at Home' programme which somebody in our far-off capital decided would be a great fillip for folks who couldn't travel to Cannes or the Riviera this year. It was a real bonus for the likes of us who hadn't even realised that you could go anywhere further than Tynemouth or Whitley Bay for the day so we descended, with every other urchin from miles around, on the big Marquee the troupe had erected in Smith's Park. Sat on hard benches under this great canopy, we scrunched up closer and closer till just about every resident from the upper and lower Ridges had piled in. You could tell the lower Ridges ones because they were the ones who wore their jumpers back to front and looked dead poor. Eventually a man with a fair isle jumper (on the right way) and baggy pants jumped on the stage and asked 'Is everybody HAPPY' and nobody said no and then he told these fantastic jokes like when is a door not a door, before another man in a fair isle jumper started pounding away on this piano as we all roared our way through the mandatory sing song. Then more excitement as kids went in the balloon blowing up race, then a skipping competition and a game where they spilled water they were supposed to be balancing on their heads and didn't even get hit by their Ma.

This frenzy of excitement and entertainment climaxed when the first fair isle man called for volunteers to sing something for the relaxed and appreciative audience. At this, everybody sat and looked at everybody else, wondering who would be brave or foolhardy enough to get up in front of this huge crowd. The embarrassed silence was broken by a few tentative claps which soon built to resounding roar of applause as the audience spotted the urchin-like figure of none other than cousin John McDonald, walking towards the stage. Dressed in sagging socks, scuffed shoes a tattered jumper and sporting that terrible Ridges haircut of a fringe in front and bald everywhere else, he confidently whispered his selection to the fair isle jumper at the piano while the Master of Ceremonies waited to give him the big intro. Our little family group sat and looked at each other in stunned disbelief as it was common knowledge John was absolutely and irreversibly tone deaf. Undeterred by this minor disability, he plunged into a rendition of *The White Cliffs of Dover* the likes of which had never been heard before or since. The

COUNTY BOROUGH OF TYNEMOUTH

PROGRAMME

FOR YOUR "HOLIDAYS AT HOME"

FROM 18th JUNE TO 18th JULY

OPEN-AIR DANCING

TYNEMOUTH PARK	SMITH'S PARK	NEW YORK
Mondays - Wednesdays - Saturdays 7-30 to 10 p.m.	Tuesdays - Fridays 7-30 to 10 p.m.	26th & 30th June - 5th & 12th July 7-30 to 10 p.m.
R.A.F. BROADCASTING BAND (In Public Shelter—if wet)	N. MOUTREY AND HIS HAWAIIAN SWINGTET (Wet or Fine!)	J. F. HALL AND HIS ORCHESTRA (In Schoolroom)

FIRST-CLASS VARIETY CONCERTS

BY "THE HOTSPURS" — "THE KING JESTERS" — "THE TYNESIDE MUMMERS" — "THE HEATONIANS"

SMITH'S PARK	NEW YORK
Every THURSDAY at 7 p.m.	23rd June and 14th July, at 7 p.m.
(Wet or Fine)	(In SOCIAL CLUB)

BAND PERFORMANCES

TYNEMOUTH PARK — Every Sunday at 7 p.m.

Popular Selections by the Best Bands in the North   (In Public Shelter—if wet)

GRAND AMUSEMENT FAIR   "FOR ALL FROM 9 TO 90!"

COLLINGWOOD VIEW FIELD—From 18th June to 3rd July

EXTRA SPECIAL ATTRACTIONS

WATCH YOUR "EVENING NEWS" EACH NIGHT FOR SPORTS, DISPLAYS, GALAS, Etc.
Printed Programmes Available (Price 2d. each)

DAILY TENNIS, GOLF, BOWLS, BOATING, SKATING, SWIMMING, SWINGS AND PONY-RIDING IN PLAYING FIELDS

RECO BROS. EMPIRE CIRCUS — MARINA AVENUE (RIDGES)

From 5th to 10th JULY

A 'Holidays At Home' poster for July 1943.

pianist tried every key except the one to their Bedford truck, the audience squirmed, the MC tried to put on his 'Isn't he a brave little chap' face and we tried to look as if we'd never seen him before. It's not generally known that the observation that 'War is Hell' was first expressed at this recital.

And so after this last assault on our battered senses, the war wound down to an end. Ships sirens wailed, rescue rockets split the sky, flares hung in the air and the church bells would have rung at The Ridges Mission if they'd had any. We went into a great round of victory parties where kids sat at long trestle tables stuffing their faces with home-made cakes and mugs of tea beneath lines of Union Jacks or anything else that fluttered like a flag. The surrounding countryside had been scoured for anything flammable as we assembled bonfires that climbed ten and twelve and fifteen feet high as we strove to be bigger than the one in the next street. Night seemed to take forever to fall but it eventually did and many hands applied matches and lighters to the paper we'd saved for this very purpose. And soon the flames flickered and flamed and finally roared into a huge conflagration that forced the happy faces further and further back from the intense heat. Then it was time for the wife up the street to set herself down at the piano that the blokes had dragged down from Mrs Wilkinson's and launch into *Knees Up Mother Brown* and *When The Boys Come Home Again*. Long past their normal bedtime, the kids sat and watched the fire die to a molten red glow as the songs quietened down, the mums had a last cigarette and one couple caused many a nudge by getting up to dance.

Soon the husbands and brothers and fathers would start to return and some 'uncles' would leave hurriedly for fresher fields. The lamps would be relit and we'd sit under them and marvel at where the swarms of moths had been through all the dark years. We learned the rare pleasure of being able to gawp into other people's now blackout curtainless windows and I remember being really surprised when Wor Ma drew ours so people couldn't do the same to us. It would be longer still before we'd be able to get back on the beaches or climb around the rocks collecting the willicks (whelks to none Geordies) that had proliferated undisturbed for the past six years. The council men came to unearth our now dank and deserted shelter and the front seemed bare and featureless without it. The communal stirrup pump remained in our possession, probably as a sort of reward for looking after it and it gradually rusted out its days in the back garden. The only sirens heard now were those from the shipyards as they summoned the faithful to work and released them at the end of the day. And so you could say that the world returned to normal although for us kids, the last six years had been as normal as they come.

War always throws up its special heroes and certainly the returned servicemen deserved the medals they showed to their loved ones before burying them in the family keepsake tin with their memories and penny policies. But none were more deserving of heroic status than the womenfolk who so calmly and phlegmatically endured the sorts of perils we can only imagine today.

Dad took sick in late 1941. His condition quickly worsened and by early 1942 he was terminally ill. He discharged himself from Preston Hospital and Wor Ma cared for him until he died in February of that year. Aged just 32, she was left with four children, two of whom were in Moor Park Hospital at the time. I was the eldest having just turned nine. If they'd given her and every other Ma a special Victoria Cross, it would have been no more than she and all of them deserved. Even if they were 'just' women.

Victory tea parties in North Shields.

SECTION SIX

WORK IS A FOUR LETTER WORD

Paddle Tugs at North Shields between the wars.

Wor Ma always used to say that a hard day's work never killed anybody and she was probably right although, in my long and varied experience, I never saw it perform any miracle cures either. Despite this somewhat jaundiced observation, it has to be said that our generation was firmly committed to the work ethic and was prepared to consider almost anything legal in the search for a hard-earned quid.

Everybody wanted to be an errand lad because you became the recipient of a company bike which was every bit as prestigious as today's company car. Not every store offered home deliveries and competition for these jobs was so intense that you usually had to be a relative of the manager to earn the privilege of delivering groceries or meat to the burghers of Tynemouth or Preston Grange. In retrospect, there was nothing particularly appealing about pushing a heavily-laden conveyance up some hill into the teeth of a force nine gale and torrential rain but this was more than compensated for when you got to take the bike home and perform wheelies and kerb jumps in front of your envious and cycle-less mates. Nobody at our end of Silkeys Lane ever got his own delivery bike but my mate 'Fatty' Jamieson had one for a while. He wouldn't let anybody ride it solo but he'd transport me in the front basket, legs dangling on either side while my bum only just cleared the wobbly little front wheel. And just imagine, the lucky recipient also got ten bob in wages as well.

I delivered papers because this remained legal long after William Wilberforce got rid of most other forms of slavery. My first job with Renton's paper shop on Albion Road was primarily intended to make a man of me but it also paid the princely sum of eight shillings a week of which I got to keep a whole two bob to fritter away on myself.

All I had to do, in return for this largesse, was to turn up six mornings a week at some unearthly hour to collect a canvas bag full of *Daily Expresses* for the toffs, *Daily Mirrors* for the workers and *Heralds* for those who had three threepenny doubles and a treble on Templegate's racing selections for the day. Hoisting this onto my puny shoulders I'd head off into the drizzle that fell whenever it wasn't snowing. My run covered a maze of streets between Ralph Gardiner and Queen Victoria Schools, all older terraces and all with letter boxes that were rusted or had springs on them that would have trapped a grizzly bear. Each paper had to be carefully extricated from the bag, folded and fed through these narrow apertures making sure that (a) each house got the paper of their choice, (b) not one drop of rain got anywhere near it, and (c) the paper was not creased crushed or damaged in any other way. Having performed these relatively simple tasks, I'd wend my way back through the early morning gloom to the garage alongside the shop where my bag was left ready to be refilled for the afternoon delivery of *Evening Chronicles* and *Shields Evening News*. And all this for ten pence a week. Six papers at three ha'pence

Albion Road. The lane between the buildings on the left led to the old converted stable where I chopped and bundled.

each plus a penny for delivery. No wonder the customers expected top service.

The good news was that there weren't any afternoon deliveries on a Sunday. The bad news was that everybody in Shields loved the much heavier and more prolific Sunday papers and my bagful would have tested the capabilities of an Olympic clean and jerk champion. Even worse, my Sunday run didn't start till I got somewhere up by The Pineapple Inn by which time, despite numerous rests, I was well and truly knackered. To save my strength I'd sit on the nearest garden wall, fossick out a *Sunday Post* and bring myself up to date on the latest exploits of Oor Wullie and The Broons. Later, I'd rest again while devouring the latest scandal from the *News of the World* or the report on yesterday's United game on the back of the *Sunday Sun*. The *Sunday Dispatch* I saved till last. It had created something of a furore by publishing excerpts from *Forever Amber*, a period novel of love, lust and heaving bosoms. The only time I ever appreciated the perks of this job was when I sat on yet another garden wall and read how Amber (the hussy) allowed one of her ample breasts to cascade from her low cut gown. It made you wonder just how much further these papers could go.

In the years when I wasn't getting fabulously wealthy sticking papers through people's doors I always looked forwards, like every other kid in Shields, to Tatie Picking Week. Held sometime late in the year this special week long holiday was declared so that the local farmers could utilise the vast pool of school-aged labour to plodge through their clarty fields picking their potato crops. Every year Wor Ma packed brown paper bags full of jam sandwiches for those of us old enough to tackle this back-breaking task and every year I'd head off on my own, determined to beat the others to the highest paying job. Every year I'd knock on farm doors only to be told that they picked them all yesterday or they only grew turnips or they already had enough kids. Whatever the reason, I'd end up eating the sandwiches in some windswept ditch before returning to an empty house to which my brothers eventually returned pockets full of money and regaling us with stories about how the farmer could have used 'hundreds' of extra hands.

Having missed out on the easy pickings from the local potato fields, I was quick to grab the opportunity to earn big bucks when another friend, Ray Wilkinson, got me a job chop'n and bundl'n. Dry kindling to get the daily fire going was always at a premium and Ray's boss catered for this by buying all the offcuts from the sawmills by the river and converting them into the neat little bundles that sold for tuppence in most corner stores. His workplace was a converted stable up a cobbled backlane behind Turnbull's, Shields most prestigious taxi and funeral service who, it was said, everybody utilised twice in their lifetime, once to get to married and once again to get buried. Here, we slaved away under the sort of conditions you see in documentaries about Third World countries. The place had that not unpleasantly sappy smell that you get around freshly sawn timber and everything from the cratered concrete floor to the white enamelled light shade was inches deep in sawdust. Smack in the centre of the room, on a log stump that must have taken a thousand years to grow and a battalion of men to move, sat a piece of cast iron equipment that probably precipitated the industrial revolution.

Ray pressed the green button that set the machine in motion and caused me to jump six feet into the air as the monster CLUNK, CLUNK, CLUNKED its way to life. He then casually selected an offcut and to my horror, fed it under the chopping blade that descended to within about an inch of his unprotected fingers. Feed CLUNK, feed CLUNK, feed CLUNK, feed CLUNK till the offcut was reduced to six or seven, six inch sticks which he quickly swept into an empty basket. His hands moved like lightning as he grabbed offcuts with one hand and fed them unerringly into the monster's jaws, rapidly emptying the first basket as the second filled with sticks. My stomach turned to water as he pushed his basket of sticks to the workbench and helped me set up for my turn at the guillotine. Despite his screamed assurances, I could see the white coated doctor standing over me, sadly shaking his head as he surveyed my bloodstained and bandaged stumps and confirmed that I'd never play the piano (or pick my nose) again. Eyes averted to avoid the inevitable spurt of blood, my first piece of timber was fed in and painstakingly converted into sticks that varied from quarter inch slivers to three inch blocks. Incredibly, after ten or fifteen minutes, I got to the stage where my empty basket was slowly but surely filling with sticks which were not only about the required size but which, more importantly, were completely free of blood stains. As we wired the sticks into neat bundles, we kept a careful count, congratulating ourselves as each hundred bundles made us a shilling richer. Easy pickings.

In the spring of 1948, I walked out of Tynemouth High School and into real full-time employment. No more the odd shilling here and there from such childish activities as paper rounds, tatie picking or chopping and bundling. Here was one more little Geordie battler all ready and willing to join the great mass of unsung heroes that made England great; Your Working Class Man. He didn't have any clear idea of just exactly what his role would be in the great industrial scheme of things, content at this stage to wallow in the prestige, the privileges and the massive wealth that he'd surely accrue as a result of his new found status. No more hiding in the toilet to make myself sick with forbidden cigarettes, now I could smoke and make myself sick wherever and whenever I wanted. No more homework, no more short pants, no more early bed times, no more teachers, no more Saturday afternoons at St James' sat on the cinder track with the rest of the kids. I was fifteen and a bit, I'd arrived, I was a man!

Jobs in those days were seldom advertised, most positions being filled by somebody within the organisation 'speaking for' a friend or relative they recommended. Not long after leaving High School, somebody 'spoke for' me and I was told to report to the bloke in charge of the store in Smith's Dock at seven thirty sharp the following Monday morning. This summons led to some frantic preparations as Wor Ma took up the legs of my new bib and brace overalls that were so stiff that they could almost stand on their own. The cobbler put steel tips on my old school shoes so that I clopped around like a regular little Fred Astaire and I was now the proud owner of an army haversack that would carry my daily bait. And last, but most importantly, I had that most essential piece of equipment, my can and related tea-making paraphernalia. Only film stars and people from Tynemouth had thermos flasks so the rest of us had to make do with our cans. Stood about eight inches high, they tapered slightly from a four inch base to a narrower top and a tightly-fitting lid that doubled as a drinking cup. Most of us used the plain tin variety but there were more upmarket models of all white enamel with fancy blue piping for those who preferred the finer things in life. They had a wire handle that allowed you to hang the can from the handlebars of your bike while in transit or to swing it around when filled with the life restoring brew. The second but equally important piece of gear was the small oval shaped tin about three inches long that didn't have a special name but which served a very special and specific purpose. This little item was split into two, and sometimes three sections, sealed with tightly fitting lids. One compartment held your daily ration of tea leaves (tea bags were still thirty years away), the second held sugar which everybody used by the shovelful, and the third, for those with the top of the range model, a big glug of Nestles condensed milk. Come the lunch time buzzer, all along the length and breadth of Tyneside, tea, milk and sugar were already in the cans awaiting only the water that boiled and bubbled at every work place. This tea-making process was simple and efficient but it tended to suffer from a couple of relatively minor setbacks. I don't know whether we used special light weight tea or whether it was the shape of the cans but for some reason or other, the tea leaves always floated in a thick slick on top of the brew so that an important part of the drinking etiquette was to be able to sip and spit tea leaves at much the same time. The second problem lay with the composition of the can itself which could be easily handled while empty but which turned white hot as soon as you filled it with boiling water. If you managed to pour some tea into the lid without inflicting third degree burns to your finger ends, you were then faced with the choice of either blistering your lips while the tea was fresh and hot or waiting twenty seconds by

SMITH'S DOCK CO LTD *Shipbuilders & Engineers* NORTH SHIELDS
New drydock 709' length x 95' breadth.   Contractors: Holloway Bros. (London) Ltd.   Consultants: T. F. Burns & Partners

An advert for the well-known North Shields employer.

which time it was clay cold. Like the Japanese, this tea-making ceremony was an important part of our cultural upbringing, designed to prove that if anything was easy you wouldn't appreciate it.

And so at just after seven on that fine and momentous Monday morn, Norman slung his bait-laden haversack over his shoulder, tucked his overall legs into his socks and nonchalantly wheeled his Hercules three-speed up to the front gate and pedalled off into the sunrise with the sort of wave that Biggles effected as he took off on yet another sortie against the Hun. Watched by an admiring Mum and three bleary-eyed siblings, he was soon lost to sight as he merged with the flotilla of bikes wheeling their way past the good old Ridges Mission, under the blackened arch of the railway bridge and on to the bumpy cobbles of the Gas Yard Lane. All downhill now across Wallsend Road past the timber yards and Western School, past Victoria Street where Brian and I had made our entrances, through the last of the still awakening terraces and finally through the double gates into the entry yard with its row after row after row of rapidly-filling bicycle racks. This was it. Red faced and ready, I'd arrived.

If I'd been a bit more observant or a bit less excited, I might have noticed that not everyone seemed to share my enthusiasm to explore the hidden face of Smith's Docks. In fact in just a few months time I'd be mooching in like them, sucking on their last half inch of Woodbine and wishing it was Sunday. But not today. Today I was entering a brand new world, a world previously only peeked at from the surrounding bank tops or through invitingly half open gates. Today I was part of it, on the inside of the high glass encrusted walls. Already I could smell the river and the tar and the smoke and see the high funnels of the docked ships all painted in colours that were as instantly recognisable then as the tail fin of today's British Airways or Qantas jet. I'd spotted one or two familiar faces but generally I was alone and anonymous in the great seething sea of black jackets, navy blue overalls and grey faces that milled like some tidal surge through the narrow aisles that housed the thirty odd clocks that confirmed the entrances and exits of the keen, the lazy, the fat, the thin, the old, the young, the skilled, the unskilled, the mass of which I was now a part. A bored clerk in one of the offices alongside the clocks, gave me my number and my very own card then watched as I fed it into the mechanism that recorded for posterity that I had passed this way at 07.23 precisely on whatever date it happened to be. Within a few weeks, the seven twenty three would become seven twenty six and then creep inexorably toward the seven thirty deadline as I savoured the extra few minutes in bed before mounting my trusty steed and pedalling like a man possessed to get through the gates before the last wails of the siren faded away. On the tick of seven thirty, gatekeepers slammed the gates in the face of any latecomers firmly barring their way until just before seven forty five

Smith's Dock Pontoon in the early 1950s.

when they re-opened briefly to admit those who had 'lost a quarter'. They opened once more at three minutes to eight to admit any late latecomers before slamming shut for the last time, forcing any really late arrivals to make the long slow return trip home where they'd suffer a tongue-lashing from their wives or mothers for losing a much needed day's pay.

The happy soul who gave me my card and supervised my entry, pointed me towards a square building about four stories high and I guessed that this was where they were anxiously awaiting my arrival. The clocks and timekeeper's offices were located on the highest part of the docks so that I had to cross a short wooden bridge to enter the top floor of my building. This floor and the one below were taken up with huge drafting offices where what seemed like hundreds of blokes in collars and ties stood in cosy groups enjoying a last smoke and discussing the weekend's events before settling themselves at the forest of drawing boards. Descending the bare concrete stairwell I passed through a yawning chasm of empty shelves and smooth concrete floors, arriving finally to the very bottom floor where I made my first human contact with a kid not much older or differently attired to myself. He happily took me to the poky wee office from which the head storeman ruled over the five or six men and two or three young 'uns who dispensed the bits and pieces needed to carry out the multitude of tasks that went on in the acres of yard around us.

After taking my name and painstakingly writing it on the only piece of paper on his desk, he passed me back to my companion to show me around. As a first step in this intensive training programme, he led me to the furthest and dingiest corner of the store where he allocated me a nail on which I could hang my gear alongside that of my fellow workers. He then showed me the row upon row of shelves and the mind boggling array of nuts and bolts and rivets and tubs of tallow and grease and reams of sandpapers and emery cloths and rasps and files (including, to my astonishment, some of the bastard variety). I couldn't wait to get home and shock my mates with such a grown up swear word.

With the mini tour of the stores out of the way, my excitement moved up a couple of notches as we stepped outside for my first look at the yard itself. Past the deep dry docks where tankers and freighters sat on stacks of blackened oily sleepers that had seldom felt the warmth of the sun. Past the gangways that led into the tomb like interiors of the vessels that towered over us like great metallic buildings. Around the glowing braziers where rivets turned white hot before being gripped in long catchers tongs and inserted into their allotted holes to be hammered into place by the riveters whose machine gun like racket never stopped. Through the engineering shop as big as a football field with its blackened roof so high that you'd have struggled to reach it with a powerful rifle and just beneath it the gantry crane that crept from end to end, the driver in his lofty cabin, moving girders and drive shafts and motors over the serried ranks of machinery that filled the smooth oil spattered floor far below him. Lathes and grinders and borers and drills, all tended by boilersuited fitters who turned handles and adjusted slides and squirted another drop of lubricating oil onto spinning parts. Higher up the yard, pattern makers fashioned complicated timber templates whose outlines would be chalked onto huge metal plates which would eventually find their way into the patchwork that made up a ship's hull. Into the relative calm of the carpenters' shop where I took particular note because it was here I was supposed to end up when I turned sixteen and could start the five-year apprenticeship to turn me into a shipwright like the ones who planed and sawed and grooved and assembled the cabinets that they'd eventually install on one of the merchantmen outside. Into the painters' yard from which the painters sallied forth and added a welcome touch of colour in their white boilersuits bespattered with the red lead and battleship grey that flew everywhere as they wielded brushes on the end of huge poles from swaying trestles in a death defying act that wouldn't have been out of place in a circus. Upwards to the riggers' loft where they always seemed to be sat around in a circle, like a bunch of grizzly old elves, twisting bits of wire and fastening things to hawsers in much the same way I used to sit around when I was bored stupid trying to tie knots in the cubs. I thanked my lucky stars that I hadn't decided to be a rigger.

The time, with all this excitement, had flown by and it was almost morning tea time when we got back to the store. This gave us the chance to repair to our dark corner where the old men sipped their tea and held court as we kids listened and learned the valuable lessons that

The British Grenadier berthed in North Shields.

would help us survive within the confines of the dockyard walls. This advice was occasionally work-related but more often consisted of the helpful little hints and tips that had served them so well over the years. The best places to get your boiling water at lunch time, the warmest spots in the winter, where to pick up your firewood supplies, where to place your bet on the horses in the unlikely event that you had sixpence to spare, which of the bowler-hatted foremen to avoid and, for newies like myself, which practical jokes I could expect to have sprung on me. Every other day we had some glaky young moron at the front door looking for the long stand that he'd already spent half a day standing around for without success. Then of course there were the other imbeciles who turned up asking for left-handed hammers or striped paint or single-sided glass. But there was little chance that anyone would catch me with such obvious old chestnuts, because, let's face it, I was a High School kid.

The end of my tea and training session signalled the start of my real work day because they weren't paying me thirteen and fourpence a week to be a tourist. It would be very melodramatic to write about cruel overseers whipping and kicking us and working us till our poor little bodies could take no more, but in reality, nobody seemed to place too many demands on us and life in the stores meandered along at a steady old clip. There was usually a bit of a rush when we opened the doors at half past seven but things quietened down after that and we'd while the time away, sweeping and resweeping the same bit of floor till another customer turned up. Rash and impetuous as we undoubtedly were, we young 'uns stayed respectfully in the background while Joe or Syd or one of the other oldies strolled up to the door to pass the time of day and ascertain exactly what our visitor required. Whichever one of us was quickest then discarded his broom and followed our leader to the appropriate rack where we'd dive into the deep bunkers to dig out the required quantity of four inch rivets or three inch whitworth hexagons while Syd or Joe supervised with much muttering and double counting and licking of pencil stubs. Then back to the brushes until another client turned up or till the twelve o'clock buzzer brought an end to all this frenetic activity.

Many of the older hands used the hour long lunch break to bus or cycle home for their hot 'dinner'. My wife's Uncle Jimmy, a boilermaker and leading light in Union affairs, made the ten minute bus trip each and every day so that he could partake of his roast dinner and pudding before returning to make boilers or to do whatever else boilermakers did. We kids couldn't be bothered with any of that and after wolfing down my dozen sandwiches, I never had any problems filling-in the remaining fifty minutes. The bottom of any empty dry dock provided a popular venue for the thirty or forty a side cricket matches that attracted young and old alike. Rudimentary bats carved out by apprentice carpenters, slogged balls fashioned from rivets wrapped in electricians tape as the hobnailed fielders slithered and slid on the wet mossy floor, (because dry docks are never dry) as they tried desperately to grab the ball as it ricoched off the steeply stepped sides. At the far end of the yard, beyond the pontoon that lifted smaller vessels clear of the water, a similarly enthusiastic mob kicked a leaden leather soccer ball with steel-toed boots that drew cheers, howls and blood in about equal proportions. Dingy huts sheltered groups of card players, all stooped intently over makeshift tables as they smoked continuously, took closely-guarded peeks at the handful of greasy cards and shoved halfpennies into the mounting kitty as they bragged their way to riches or thought about the hours of overtime they'd have to work to make up their losses. The odd fisherman perched on bollards, at peace with the world as their heavily-weighted chord lines cut through the turquoise blue oily-patterned surface of the sluggishly running river.

Whether we were watching or participating, or just mooching around like lost sheep, it seemed only minutes before the siren announced once more that our precious hour had flown as quickly as it always seemed to do. The same couldn't be said for the remainder of the working day that seemed to drag on interminably. Finally, however, the clock ticked its way around to five o'clock, just fifteen minutes short of the final whistle. All over the yard, machines were switched off, braziers doused, tools carefully restored to bags and boxes and lugged to the metal locker, the store was swept yet again, and slowly but surely, the human tide that had swept in almost ten hours earlier, started to ebb inexorably toward the entry yard and the row of clocks. The rules were quite clear and strictly enforced. Nobody was allowed in that top yard until the five fifteen hooter sounded. The rules, however didn't say anything about being close to the yard and so tens and then hundreds and finally thousands, crammed in and around and beside and behind every building surrounding the yard until the first strident note broke the hushed silence. Then, like four or five 'Dark Brigades', they poured forth, not into the valley of the shadow of death but through the aisles, cards into waiting clocks, then to the bicycle yard and the beckoning gates beyond. The fastest and fittest were through the gates, heads down and bums up before the last wail had died away. In their wake a veritable avalanche of black riders forced their way through the sea of equally black pedestrians as they headed for the row of buses or the nearby streets. Unlike the morning influx which was slow and steady and quiet and almost sullen, the exit was fast and furious and good natured as they returned to wives and mothers and brothers and sisters and perhaps even a beer or two and a game of darts or dominoes later on. Somewhere in all this crush, little Norman panted and puffed and changed gears and pedalled up hill to The Ridges and the family all waiting to hear about the day's goings on. Wor Ma was bound to ask if I'd seen Mr Stutt and if I'd had enough bait and did I ever work overtime and was I tired and stuff like that while the kids would look at my oil stained (and deliberately unwashed) hands, green with envy that you could get that dirty without getting into trouble. If everyone has their two minutes of fame then surely this was mine!

Hero status, like first day nerves and excitement, soon fade and within a few weeks, Norman was almost ready to admit that he just might have been wrong. But relief was at hand. His undoubted potential had obviously been recognised by some wise, all-seeing, all-knowing power and the word had come down that on the following Monday he was to report to Head Office at the bottom of Coach Lane to take up the elevated position of Letter Lad. Seldom could any young industrialist have had such a meteoric rise to fame and fortune. Well fame anyway because there was no indication that my weekly thirteen and fourpence would be increased but my still stiff dungarees could be put away as Wor Ma ironed my white shirt and rushed off to buy half a dozen detachable collars and borrow a tie from one of the neighbours. No good being one of the office toffs if you didn't look the part.

Not long after taking on my daily letter run, I found myself with an internal memo addressed to the foreman of the rigging department, one spot I hadn't visited since that first tour of the yard. Reclimbing the stairs to their elevated erie, I squeezed my way through the narrow door into the dim and tarry smelling interior. Adjusting my eyes to the gloom, I spotted the usual group of riggers sat around like so many elves, splicing or binding or whatever it was that so preoccupied them. The bloke nearest me had a pleasantly amiable face and he nodded affably, but a little vaguely, as I asked him the way to the foreman's office. When I repeated my question, he cupped his ear and answered that no he didn't know where the doorman was. Clearing my throat, I repeated my initial question, making sure that I spoke just a bit louder and enunciating as clearly as I could. This had absolutely no effect as he cupped his ear a bit harder and stared intently at me as he explained apologetically how 'He was just a bit deaf with all the noise you know and could I just speak a little bit louder.' Taking the deepest of deep breaths, I shouted my request yet again only to be met with more 'Eh's?' and 'What's that's?' as I got closer and closer to the cupped ear and screamed louder and louder till my throat ached. Swallowing hard and bracing myself for one last despairing effort, it suddenly dawned on me that all the other riggers were sat back wearing expressions of pure and unadulterated joy. Like so many before and so many more to come, I'd been well and truly caught. Every time I revisited the riggers loft from that day on, I was greeted with huge smiles, callused hands cupped over oily ears, and a chorus of 'What's that's?' and 'Where's the doorman then?' So much for a High School education.

Late in 1948, I forsook the excitement of Smith's for a career in art and advertising. My new employers didn't have thousands of employees or acres of ground. They didn't even have a reception area or a commissionaire. In fact Rogers and Smythe, only had Rogers and Smythe and the small downstairs flat at No 40 Howard Street that housed their recently established partnership. Albert Smythe, the older of the two, was a canny, pipe-smoking man who was quite well known in local amateur art circles. He always wore a khaki coloured dust coat with a belt, never raised his voice and was the practical half of the company. David Rogers was much younger, much more modern and extroverted and full of grand ideas which Albert responded to with much head nodding and pipe lighting. If he'd been born forty years later he would undoubtedly have been a marketing manager or one of those advertising gurus who run concepts up flagpoles. It didn't take me too long to familiarise myself with my new workplace. The varnished front door, complete with a posh brass nameplate that David's Mum polished regularly, led into a passage that went straight through to another pea green planked door that opened into the crumbling back yard and the ancient outside toilet with its much scrubbed wooden seat and a bird's nest under the front eaves. If you sat quietly enough you could listen to the sparrows coming and going and chirruping away to each other as if you were out in the wild Northumbrian moors instead of a hundred yards from the bus stops in Northumberland Square. Two rooms of about equal size, led off to the left of the passage and the first of these was where most of the action took place. A huge ornate fireplace that was never used, served as a reminder of the days when this had been the living room of an up and down terrace. The big bay window that looked out onto Howard Street was glazed with frosted glass so that the regular procession of passers by couldn't gawp through it as they wandered past on their way to and from the Square. This window space was Albert's domain as he worked away here on a huge old kitchen table with carved legs and a knife

Howard Street with the old library clock on the left corner. I worked at Rogers & Smythe, about a hundred yards further up on the left.

drawer that held all his bits and pieces. David worked at the other end of the room on a flash drawing board that was as high tech as anything you'd see around Shields in those days and I sometimes got to rule a few lines on it as he lit another Capstan Full Strength and supervised my efforts, a bit like the King letting one of the kids have a few minutes on the throne. The back room was cold and bare and empty apart from the silk screen table stuck in the centre, a few cans of printing ink and a pile of old newspapers plus a ten gallon drum of turps for cleaning up.

The business survived on a small but steady output of the small cards and tickets that local businesses used to advertise their wares. Most of these cards were about ten by four inches, all done by hand to promote Saville Studios photographic expertise, the merits of Brittain's fine furniture, the quality of Mahoney's vegetables, the cures on hand at Hogg's the chemist and a hundred and one others. My initial responsibilities consisted mainly of wandering the town for pipe tobacco or cigarettes for the bosses and searching through the pile of old magazines for the pictures that adorned the finished cards. Brides for the frock shops, wedding cakes for the bakers, bunches of flowers, fancy furniture, hats for the milliners, fish for Hadaway's – I soon became so expert that I could dig out and cut out an appropriate picture in no time. As I became more skilled my duties expanded to cutting the cards, then pasting the pictures into place and ultimately to painting the red or black border that finished off each work of art. A regular little Michelangelo. The cards themselves were displayed in post offices, telephone boxes, shop windows, buses, and just about anywhere else that the advertisers thought might bring in a bit more business. Madison Avenue, it most certainly wasn't but I loved every minute of it as the three of us chatted and smoked and cut and painted and pasted. Sometimes we'd get a huge order for maybe twenty or thirty posters to announce a forthcoming sale at D. Hill Carters or one of our other finer establishments. This sent David rushing to the back room where he'd take up his surgical blade and quickly prepare the stencil and set up the screen table where he splashed ink and dragged a big rubber squeegee while I flew around pegging the finished posters onto the lines that criss-crossed the room till it looked just like Wor Ma's on a wash day.

I loved that job so much that I used to stay back way beyond my normal hours just pottering around, practising my borders or chewing the fat with the bosses. Wor Ma never saw it as a 'proper job' and she used to worry about what sort of future I'd have cutting and pasting pictures on to bits of card. She also worried that my twenty-five shillings starting wage showed every sign of also being my finishing wage despite vague promises about a bit more as the business grew which in truth it never looked like doing. I believe in fact that there must have been many weeks when I earned more than the bosses especially after young David talked Albert into opening an art supply shop at the top of Bedford Street. Truth to tell, Albert didn't need too much coercing as all his friends in the local art society were really enthusiastic and talked about how the town 'really needed a top quality establishment' to look after them. This shop was even more of a treasure trove than Howard Street and I spent many a happy hour fossicking through the treasure trove of Windsor Newton oils, Reeve's watercolours, pots of poster paint, packets of plasticine, jugs full of squirrel hair and sable brushes, palettes, canvasses, special boards and all sorts of fancy art papers. That shop had everything. Everything, that is, except customers. Sure the local artists did frequent the place but how often do you need another tube of burnt sienna or a half inch flat sable?

Many of the few who did cross the threshold were those looking to take advantage of our photo colouring and framing expertise. Colour films were still many years away so we had a regular flow of folk looking to have their drab black and white wedding photographs turned into glowing colour. I got to be quite the little expert at converting these family artworks from drab greys to hideously coloured frocks, bright yellow hair, even brighter blue eyes and faces that ranged between pale pink and vividly apoplectic. The finished products, even to my young and untrained eyes, always looked garish and horrible and I used to hold my breath when the customer turned up to pick up their framed and finished order but, despite my apprehension, they invariably looked thrilled to bits and rushed off to hang them in a place of honour in their front room. I worked out afterwards that our clientele must have consisted largely of folk who in later years would have a great collection of those Charles and Diana souvenir tea towels and clocks and plates where they both smile at you with eyes that are so crossed that they look every which way at the same time.

Wor Ma's mutterings had grown as time passed and they grew even louder as my sixteenth birthday came and went without any sign of an increase in their business or in my wages. Her prods became positive pushes when the local labour exchange wrote advising me that one of the new factories on the trading estate was looking for a 'photostat operator', a position for which they felt I would be eminently suitable. I ignored her nagging and the next missive that arrived but it was more than my life was worth to ignore the third that saw me walking the ten minutes up Norham Road to see what they had to offer and to find out exactly what the hell a photostat operator did. The factory was one of a number that were being built on the new Trading Estate as part of some government scheme to bring new industries to the North East, and it was far and away the biggest of the newcomers with its three stories of offices fronting Norham Road while the factory behind stretched over half a mile along the busy Coast Road that carried the buses and other

Norman outside 9 Laburnum Avenue when he was in his twenties. Norman in exactly the same spot in 1994.

traffic to and from Newcastle. A sort of grassy moat ran along the length of the offices and I had to cross a nifty concrete bridge to make my way into the ultra-modern entry foyer and front up to the inevitable commissionaire. In fact this mob were so up-market and modern that they actually had not one but two commissionaires, this one and one of lower rank who looked after the more mundane factory gates. When I got to know him better I'd discover that he, like my old friend at Smith's, was also a Jim and I'd probably have gone through life convinced that all commissionaires were Jims were it not for the fact that the bloke on the tradesman's gate was Bill.

Stomping off in a flurry of swinging arms and polished boots, Jim left me to compare these modern surroundings with the ancient splendour of Smith's Docks and the two rooms of Rogers and Smythe. The foyer, by modern standards, was quite plain and unpretentious but I was most impressed with the feature wall of glass blocks that extended from the lower floor, through the foyer and up to the floor above. All blue and brilliant, I felt something like a fish would feel if it suddenly found itself trapped in an iceberg. My musings were cut short as CSM Jim marched me along a passage and into the presence of the Personnel Manager. My shock introduction to the twentieth century was completed when I found my interviewer to be a lady would you believe, and this in an age when the most senior executive positions held by any other woman in Shields was as conductress on the number six bus. She smilingly explained what the job entailed, all of which was quickly forgotten when she got to the important bit about how it paid no less than two pounds five shillings a week, a full quid more than I was currently earning. My mind raced as I tackled the ethical dilemma of what was more important, a job in which I was happy and fulfilled or a lousy extra half a crown a week, which is what I'd end up with after paying Wor Ma her board. Not wishing to appear cheap or easily bought, I waited a full five seconds before accepting and heading back to Howard Street to hand in my notice.

The company that had so shamelessly headhunted me, was reputedly the largest furniture factory in Europe at that time and its sole objective seemed to be to churn out as many bits of furniture as it could in the shortest possible time. Secondary considerations like aesthetics and quality didn't rate terribly highly and as long as the pieces of furniture stood up and looked glossy they were loaded on to one of the fleet of trucks that rushed them to the company stores dotted all around the country. My official duties consisted of working around the design office and operating the photostat machine, a sort of pre-historic photo copier. Unofficially, I spent a large proportion of each day searching for the Senior Service cigarettes which the chief designer smoked none-stop.

My eighteenth birthday came and so did the pink papers that requested my presence in His Majesty's Armed Forces for the next two years. I'd return in 1953 by which time the Army had made a man of me but it was never the same. My boss had changed but the wages hadn't. My cousin John, who worked across the Coast Road at the Formica factory 'spoke for me' and I shocked my mother-in-law to-be by giving up my collar and tie (and four quid a week) for a set of overalls and about three times as much. This was to be the end of my excitement era – as the next time I changed jobs was 1988 by which time I'd moved to the other side of the world and finally managed to get back into a collar and tie yet again. Which only goes to prove that some people will do anything for a dollar.

SECTION SEVEN

THAT'S ENTERTAINMENT

The Central Palace in Saville Street West. It later became The Comedy.

What did you do before TV Daddy? Now there's a question that has been asked of us at least once, and one that we oldies ask ourselves every few years. The more nostalgic of us tend to go on about how romantic it was and how we all used to amuse ourselves in a million and one ways. According to them, we chattered over dinner like a regular bunch of Noel Cowards before adjourning to the parlour where we'd all have such a jolly time playing charades until father sat down at the pianoforte and we harmonised our way through the latest Anne Zeigler and Webster Booth medley. In reality of course it was nothing like that. Dinner conversations at our place usually consisted of 'Get your elbows off the table' or 'Is there any more?' while our musical talents only ever got dusted off on New Year's Eve when a choir of relaxed and slightly inebriated uncles harmonised their way through 'Nellie Dean' and cousin Joe took Kathleen home again across the ocean wild and wide. The kids played their indoor games for the fortnight they lasted after Christmas then spent the other fifty weeks reading or listening to the radio, watching the still black and white images flickering across the silver screen or very, very occasionally visiting 'The Theatah'.

The highlight of our theatrical year was undoubtedly the annual pilgrimage to far-off Newcastle to see whatever pantomime was playing at the Empire Theatre. This was as much a part of our Christmas break as the trees and stockings and it involved all the organisation and planning of your average polar expedition. The four of us were scrubbed, our shoes polished, our hair flattened with a combination of heavy brushing and Wor Ma's spit, our top coats neatly fastened and a hanky pinned to one sleeve before we were finally inspected and pronounced fit to set off along West Percy Road for the Square where we'd stand hopping impatiently from foot to foot till the number eleven drew up to our stop. The half hour journey flew by and in what seemed like a twinkling, we were clattering back down the twisty stairs and out into the Haymarket with its serried ranks of bus ramps and cosy-looking cafes where bus crews drank huge mugs of tea and filled the already steam-filled interiors with even denser clouds of cigarette smoke. Clutching hands in a nervous little chain and never more than one pace away from Wor Ma, we scuttled off knowing full well that we'd probably never be found again if we got separated in this busy alien land.

Shortly afterwards, all red-faced and sweaty despite the grey winter morning, the last road was crossed, the last corner rounded and there, right in front of us, stood that most imposing of all local theatres – The Empire. Brightly lit signs heralded forthcoming attractions, coloured bulbs reflected in adjacent windows and off the usually wet roadway and great arched doors led into a brightly-lit foyer that was guarded by a chucker out in a burgundy tail coated uniform that would not have been out of place on a Ruritanian field marshall. By-passing all this opulence we headed instead for a long dim alleyway, where a small faded sign pointed almost apologetically to the battered green doors at the far end which would eventually admit us to what was officially described as the upper circle but which to everyone else was the Gods. Despite the fact that it was still just mid-morning, families of harassed mums and excited kids already filled half the passageway and we dragged Wor Ma bodily along the narrow passage, determined to stake our claim in the queue and settle ourselves for the long, long wait.

A local clock chimed the fifteen minutes at what seemed to us like every hour. The queue gradually built up and squashed us closer and closer together until we were packed like a football crowd between the high grey walls. An occasional slurry of sleety rain scythed down the narrow concrete canyon, causing us to huddle even closer together like a mob of border sheep sheltering from the wind that flew almost unnoticed over our heads. And still they turned up until the queue stretched all the way to the end of the passage and then out onto the busy pavement and Wor Ma and the neighbouring womenfolk, who were now on first name terms, congratulated themselves for getting there in plenty time.

Wor Ma – Alice Christenson.

The tedium was relieved about midday when one of our neighbours undertook to 'keep our place' and we pushed and wormed our way out of the queue and into the shorter one, just up the street, that would shortly deposit us in Fenwick's 'Caffee' as we always insisted on calling it. This was almost as exciting as the show as a stiffly-starched waitress led us through the maze of tables until we were sat around our own crackly starched table cloth on which sat cut glass salt and pepper shakers and fancy sauce bottles just like you saw in pictures of the King and Queen at the Lord Mayor's banquet. Wor Ma, when the waitress arrived to take our order, put on the sort of voice she adopted when she was talking-to the doctor as she ordered a pot of tea, a big plate of chips and, if we were really flush, a serving of their very best sausages. Sneaking looks to see how everybody else behaved and which knives they used and how they held their tea strainers, we'd smother the delicious repast in HP sauce and hoe into it as genteelly as we could, bearing in mind Wor Ma's stage whispered admonitions to sit up straight, not to lick the top of the sauce bottle and of course keep our elbows firmly by our sides, a not inconsiderable feat when you're trying to spear the last slippery chip. When we'd drained the last drop of tea, fought over the last chip, dipped the last piece of margarined bread into the last smear of brown sauce, Wor Ma signalled the waitress with an imperious wave as if we did this every day of the week.

Then back to the laneway where we'd fight our way back through the throng to renew acquaintances with our smiling place-keepers. Suddenly, the head of the queue seemed to come alive. People stirred and stretched arms skywards, those sat on bags and baskets, stood up stamping feet and pulling their clothes straight, women checked their purses for the umpteenth time, kids the length of the alley asked yet again was it time and everywhere groups gathered themselves expectantly together. And then, with a great metallic clang, the doors flew inwards and we were bathed in the light at the end of the tunnel that we've been looking for ever since.

Gathering up kids and coats and shopping bags and umbrellas and assorted paraphernalia, the mob shuffled slowly but surely towards the doors, the chatter becoming more animated as we neared them and then dying away as we finally reached the bare-painted entry where Wor Ma dug through her purse till she had enough coins to pay for one and four halves. Then full steam ahead up the bare concrete stairs that kept doubling back on themselves, past barred doors that led into dress circles and other posh levels until finally, all puffing and panting, to the usherette who tore our tickets in half and waved us through to our final destination. And more waiting.

Eventually, the other levels started to fill at a trickle and then in a steady flow as the big clock ticked closer and closer to starting time. Kids yelled and pointed as the fire screen was enveloped behind huge scarlet curtains all fringed with miles of gold embroidery and bedecked with loops of gold ropes and massive tassels. The air thickened with a mixture of expectancy and Woodbine smoke as warning bells sounded in some far off foyer and usherettes waved torches and scurried faster and faster as they sat the latecomers. More nudging and pointing as the musicians filed nonchalantly into the orchestra pit where they rifled through sheet music and blew stridently discordant notes on gleaming brass instruments. Then the house lights dimmed and the great man himself ducked from under the stage, mounted his podium and bowed deeply as the spotlight glared on the shining tail coat that outglistened his Brylcreamed hair. Waiting till the rapturous applause had died down, he tapped his baton against the top of his lectern, raised both arms in the manner of Christ of the Andes, then swept the orchestra off into the overture as each musician competed valiantly to see who would finish first. Then the curtains opened to a chorus of 'Oohs' and 'Aahs'.

After the grey Novocastrian streets and the subdued theatre house lights, the stage stood out like an island of light and colour. Brilliant floodlights highlighted the radiant colours of the Giant's castle or Aladin's cave or the London street down which Dick Whittington and his five foot six cat would shortly stride. Scything spotlights swept over the audience's head, changing moods and colours as operators swivelled tinted lenses that turned our pale expectant faces red and blue and green in rapid succession. Then the huge cheer as the Dame, usually played by some well known male comedian, emerged from stage left, all done up in curly wig, voluminous crinolined dress and more makeup than the rest of the cast combined. Mincing and prancing 'she'd' fall over at least half a dozen times in the first minute, each time revealing the frilly knickers that would bring forth a huge roar on each of the hundred or so occasions 'she' chose to flaunt them throughout the rest of the show. An even greater roar threatened to bring down the massive chandelier as Tom, Dick or Jack or whoever the hero was, bounded on from stage right. Usually played by a magnificently buxom blonde, she'd stride bravely to centre stage where she'd come to a stop, hands on hips, legs akimbo and chest extended to its most impressive maximum as she beamed a smile that was brave and boyish to us but which might just have had a somewhat different effect on the few males lucky enough to radiate in it. The music grew solemn and mournful as she went into a short monologue about the hardships 'his' family faced and how 'he', although only a lad, would restore the family fortune and thwart that dastardly villain Sir Jasper Snottly. No sooner were the words out of her mouth than this nasty piece of work made his first appearance, ignoring our heart felt boos as he leered and sneered and twirled his black moustache in a shameless display of heartless malevolence.

All we had to do from here on in was to sit on the edge of our seats as the Dame fell over and sang funny songs, the cat or the cow or the horse did all sorts of fancy tricks accompanied by funny noises from the drummer, the villain plotted fiendish plots and our hero continued to stick out her ample chest and overcome them all. Somewhere around about the third act there'd be a bit where we kids had to affirm that we all believed in fairies which shouldn't have been too hard when you consider that most of the cast were appearing in drag. Finally, with evil overcome and our hero and his or her family restored to their rightful place in the social strata, the whole cast filled the stage for the grand finale. Cats cavorted, mice marched, well-endowed matelots did hip shaking hornpipes, the villain skulked, the dame showed her knickers for the hundred and first time and our hero stood centre stage waving straight at us. The curtain fell and rose and fell and rose yet again as we stomped and clapped and cheered and envied those who could put their fingers in their mouths and whistle. Then inevitably, the curtain fell down and stayed down, the orchestra struck up the national anthem and we all asked God to save the King because after all he was in charge and look what a marvellous afternoon he'd given us.

Being transported once a year left plenty time for other cultural activities and our most common escape route was between the covers of whatever we could lay our hands on to read. Like most kids of that era, my introduction to the beauty and poetry of the written word came not from Shakespeare or Dostoyevski but from the pages of the weekly comics that we read and re-read and swapped and traded till they hung in tatters. We took endless hours of enjoyment from the *Beano* and the *Dandy* and the wonderful assortment of characters that filled their pages. Pansy Potter (the strongman's daughter); Keyhole Kate whose long pointy nose was always stuck in somebody else's business; Desperate Dan and his huge cow pies with the horns sticking up through the crust; Lord Marmaduke (Snooty to you) and his gang; Billy Bunter who peered short-sightedly through his granny glasses and said things like 'Oh Lor' and 'You rotter'; Our Ernie whose Da puffed on his pipe and always said 'Daft I calls it' in the last square of every cartoon adventure; Dennis the Menace and his sister Beryl the Peril and so many more, some of whose names and faces now escape me but all of whom gave great value for the tuppence we scrounged for each weekly edition.

There was also, of course, the *Film Fun* and the *Radio Fun* which starred the personalities we watched or listened to at the time. While they were never quite as popular as the main two they were still much sought after so that we could catch up with the latest misadventures of our favourite film stars like Old Mother Riley (who was really a bloke in drag) and his daughter Kitty who in real life was his wife. Radio was at its peak, except in our house where we could never get one that worked, and stars like Tommy Handley shared the pages with Flanagan and Allen, who were my Dad's favourites, Kenneth Horne and Richard Murdoch who sang *Much Binding In The Marsh* (tiddly om pom pom) forever and a day and of course Arthur Askey who wore funny hats and sang a song about bumble bees and who eventually became a legend in his own lifetime without ever doing anything funny that I saw.

As we grew up and turned into discerning adolescents, we graduated from the pictures in the *Dandy* and *Beano* to the more mature and sophisticated stories in the *Wizard*, the *Hotspur* and the *Adventure*.

Every comic had one regular called something like Roy of the Rovers who week after week kicked or headed or otherwise engineered the winning goal just as the ref was raising his whistle to blow full-time. They should have called him Last Minute Lou or Gordon the Gong as he must have accumulated more cup winners' medals than the people who made them but no he was just plain Roy and we couldn't wait to see how he'd save Rovers yet again. Just as inevitably each week, a baffled Scotland Yard was forced to enlist the aid of that super sleuth Sexton Blake to solve the latest baffling murder case. With his curved pipe smoking away in one hand and his trusty magnifying glass in the other, our tweed-caped and deerstalker-hatted hero invariably uncovered the vital clue that led unerringly to the butler. Despite the fact that most of the comics were sold to kids who had to beg borrow or steal the few pence they cost, they invariably had at least one regular character whose life style was as alien as if he'd come from Jupiter or Mars. Like Cripple Dick Archer who went to an absolutely splendid public school where they talked about Stimpson minor and

Stimpson major, where the juniors were called fags and where they ate hot buttered crumpet in the common room and where they carried him shoulder high across the quadrangle after he hit the winning run off the beastly fast bowler from St Snodgrass. And all this for kids who lived on The Ridges and drank tea from jam jars!

The transition from comics to 'proper' books was accommodated via the auspices of the junior library that sat just across the road from it's big brother in Howard Street. Here I'd burrow my way between the closely stacked shelves in search of the latest William book. God knows how many stories Richmal Crompton penned about this cheeky school boy with his cap askew, his grazed knees his socks perpetually around his ankles and a disarming grin on his grubby countenance. However many she wrote (and I was a ripe old age before I learned that Richmal was a woman) I read them all, many of them more than once. From here it was an easy transition to the ripping yarns that crammed the shelves. Every week seemed to bring a brand new Biggles adventure to enthral us, and when there wasn't, we still had the works of Percy F. Westerman, Edgar Rice Burroughs, H. Rider Haggard and so many more. Then there were the real classics as the Squire and Jim 'Awkins calmly faced up to the dastardly deeds of Blind Pew and Long John Saliva and his parrot and the rest of their cut throat crew. And what about *Kidnapped* and *King Solomon's Mines* and the sheer terror of that bit where Marley's horrible apparition appeared in the dim dark interior of Scrooge's bedroom.

When we weren't reading books, many of us spent our evenings crouched over the radio although our lot missed out on this for many years due to the fact that we seldom had a set that actually worked. We had plenty that whistled and crackled and picked up what sounded very much like the German High Command, but not many that got anything as mundane as the BBC. Most of them came from a second hand shop at the bottom of Camden Street where Wor Ma would part with a pound or two of her hard earned on a 'renovated' model that usually spent more time on the bus and in the back of the shop than it ever did in our front room. The lack of an efficient receiving system put us at a constant social disadvantage as we were forced to stand and look intelligent while our neighbours raved on about how funny Tommy Handley was the night before. These problems were finally overcome when the men strung cables from house to house and connected us to the magic of Rediffusion which, for a few bob a week brought us the BBC and their toffee-nosed announcers as clear as a bell.

Of course you didn't have to be at home to enjoy the radio. At ten thirty each day we had *Music While You Work* and at twelve thirty on the dot we had the choice of listening to *Workers' Playtime* on odd days and *Works Wonders* on Tuesdays and Thursdays. *Workers' Playtime* was the professional lunch time offering where 'stars of stage, screen and radio' sang or whistled or told jokes or did whatever else had made them famous. They invariably included somebody who played *The Flight Of The Bumblebee* on a mouth organ, a soprano who sang *Oh For The Wings, For The Wings Of A Dove* and someone who specialised in excruciatingly bad animal impressions. *Works Wonders* was transmitted from some of the huge factories that England had before Maggie Thatcher closed them all down to improve the economy. The workers themselves provided the 'entertainment' which generally included a bloke who sang Jerusalem in the key of S, a comedian who was funnier than John Major and a ventriloquist who talked about drinking 'gottles of geer'. Some of these acts did go on to become world famous lathe operators.

While comics and books and radio and music played a reasonably important part in our lives, we were first, second, third and last the generation of cinema goers. The pictures were a way of life that we studied and enjoyed and debated with all of the intensity and enthusiasm that they undoubtedly deserved. Shields, in those halcyon days had no less than six thriving cinemas plus The Carlton at Tynemouth, two more at Whitley Bay, another at Monkseaton, The Lyric in Howdon and at least a dozen more for those prepared to pay the one and fourpence return to Newcastle and back. Our six local establishments provided a wide range of refuges to which we regularly escaped from the often harsh reality outside their doors. The Princes (or Gaumont), smack in the middle of Shields and next door to the railway station was by far our poshest and most prestigious establishment. With its carpeted floors, heavy velvet drapes, wurlitzer organ and ornate decor, this was definitely the top of our picture going market. It was here that we sang along with the Saturday morning GB club and here that the better heeled gigolos forked out all of two bob a seat to impress their intendeds and to lord it over us peasants in the stalls below. In those boom times we invariably had to queue under the long awning that kept the worst of the rain off us but did nothing to reduce the chill wind that cut through mackintoshes and greatcoats as if they were made of gossamer gauze. The usherette, in her smart maroon uniform, emerged every now and again to announce that there were plenty of seats in the front circle or standing room in the back circle and we'd watch, green with envy, as the odd couple decided to bugger the expense and blew the money they'd intended to save as a deposit on a trip to Blackpool on two warm seats upstairs. At even longer intervals she'd poke her Tony home-permed head into the cold to issue the glad tidings that there were two singles downstairs, at which a couple at the front decided on a trial separation or two lucky singles hopped inside. And so the queue shuffled silently and anonymously forward. Few words were spoken, people smoked cigarettes that they tried to protect in cupped hands, stamped their feet, looked at watches, if they were rich enough to own one, and wondered if they wouldn't have been better off trying The Howard where you always got in.

Every civilised cinema in the world adopted the perfectly sensible arrangement of starting their programmes at set times. When one programme was finished, they chucked everybody out and let a bundle of new people in for the next performance. There may have been the odd exception in those places where they showed non-stop newsreels or raincoat romances but generally speaking the natives went to the one o'clock or half past seven or whatever show. But of course we Shields folk never laid any claims to being unduly civilised and so we had what were laughingly described as continuous performances. This meant that the cinema opened its doors at one for the matinee and just kept cycling support film, newsreels, trailers, main film and then off again. They did advertise starting times in the *Shields Evening News* but this went very much under the classification of totally useless information as all the cinemas, apart from the most terrible of flea pits, were always full so what time you got through the door depended entirely on the length of the queue and when those inside decided they'd had enough. Some little old ladies used to turn up for the doors opening and didn't leave till bed time, spoiling everything for the poor sods stood outside and also for their neighbours by continually and deafeningly munching their way through bags of Smith's crisps and letting everybody know how the main movie ended. Unless you were extraordinarily lucky, you inevitably entered the theatre just as Sherlock Holmes was unmasking the villain that you'd never have picked in a hundred years or just as the packed court heard the confession that made the rest of the show superfluous. But these were minor setbacks and we were there every night except Sunday when it was sinful to watch movies so we stayed home and smoked and gambled instead.

The Rex was our closest cinema and I spent almost as much time inside as I did outside waiting to get in. Not the prettiest building on all of Tyneside, it stood on its own triangular block of ground a squarely unimpressive brick edifice that was probably designed by the same bloke who built the Knott's Flats. Little did we realise in those halcyon days that this huge, and hugely popular, auditorium would one day become a Bingo Hall where Wor Ma spent the twilight of her life telling the caller to 'shake his balls'. The Albion, just along the road from Christ Church, was a much smaller but cosier cinema where my bride-to-be and I spent our first nervous date in a back circle that was warm and comfortable without being anywhere as majestic and elegant as The Gaumont. From here it was literally all downhill to our older establishments.

The Albion Cinema.

The Boro at the bottom of Rudyard Street had a quite imposing entrance to the circle but a pokey little alley that admitted the peasants who could only afford the sixpence that entitled them to the discomforts of the stalls. Hard and absolutely unyielding, the seats had springs that gave them all the characteristics of the giant clam that caught the pearl diver in Pago Pago. Even worse, the upstairs circle was supported by a series of pillars which did their job extremely well but which made viewing well nigh impossible if you got anywhere behind them. As a consequence, movies at The Boro were liberally punctuated by the groans of patrons as they forced the seats down, then the sharp snap as they clamped shut as they stood and clattered through the dark to prise open another with a less interrupted view of the screen.

The Comedy Theatre was almost hidden away from view in a stretch of older shops in the middle of Saville Street and was entered through a drab passageway whose only concession to the cinematic arts was a glass case holding a handful of black and white stills and lots of dead flies. Two thirds of the way along the passage was a tiny booth from which an even tinier old woman dispensed the tickets that authorised you to mount the short flight of stairs that wound up to the darkened interior above. One of the good things about The Comedy was that you were never far from the screen as it only held a handful of people when it was full, an extremely rare occurrence as the films it showed were either so old or so terrible that even Grandma Mac steered well clear of them.

And that brings us last, and quite clearly least by a considerable margin, to The Howard or The Howard Hall as my Granda always called it. It was here on twisted and collapsing seats, worn smooth by thousands of fidgeting flannel-clad bums, that our cinematic education began. There were two generally accepted methods of gaining access to this high point on our social calendar. Law abiding types like myself usually adopted the orthodox approach of parting with the penny or tuppence that gave you legitimate access to the flea-bitten interior while less affluent and less scrupulous theatre-goers used the cheaper alternative of sneaking down the back lane that led to the fire doors through which they could squeeze into the toilets at the side the stage. This urinal had once been painted the mandatory cream and green but was now predominantly the latter colour as the walls grew a delicate form of moss in the water that seeped from the rain that lashed through the broken windows and dripped and ran from the rusted pipes that ran around its walls. It smelled just like toilets used to smell before people started throwing those crystal things in them, somewhere between the aroma of a well-rotted compost heap or a poorly cleaned stable.

Having found a seat that looked like it might survive the afternoon's screaming and squirming, we'd settle back and cheer our hearts out as a small screen emerged from behind the once blue and gold curtains.

Harbour View from Liddell Street. Notice the posters for The Boro, The Albion and The Howard at the bottom of the photograph.

The afternoon started with a fine display of flickering and flashing and upside down numbers before the tinny soundtrack soared and slowed and then hit something like the right speed as the projectionist fiddled with his primitive equipment and we launched into the cartoon. This was followed by what was undoubtedly the highlight of the afternoon – the serial. Week after week our heroes hurtled over cliffs, fell from cars, lay in front of speeding locomotives or whirring saw blades or vanished in massive explosions, always to reappear the following week, saved by divine providence or a bit of rope that we and the villain hadn't noticed.

Once the cartoons and serials were out of the way, we settled back to see what sort of cowboy movie was in store for us this week. I don't know whether it was traditional or whether The Howard had just got their hands on this job lot of cowboy films but whatever the reason, that's what we got every week. Gene Autrey battled rustlers one Saturday, Tom Mix wrestled hand-to-hand with fearsome Sioux warriors the next, then Roy Rogers protected the wagon train before the Cisco Kid sorted out the rotten cattle baron the week after. We might, on rare occasions be treated to a change as the Mounties stuck it up the Indians but generally it was our regular heroes who took centre screen. It's strange, in retrospect, but thanks to The Howard, we nine and ten-year-old Geordies knew more about Arizona than we did about Ashington.

The time eventually came when, as mature and sophisticated ten or twelve-year-olds, we outgrew such childish offerings and moved on to the more mature cinematography available elsewhere. We were lucky enough to catch the end of those magnificent British war movies in which the Germans were always as thick as two short planks and the British officers always had cute little moustaches like David Niven and always called their troops 'cheps'. Although the majority of war films covered the exploits of the lads in khaki, the other branches weren't neglected. I wouldn't miss the Air Force ones where jolly types lolled languidly around in sheepskin jackets and Old Etonian scarves, curling their long moustaches and saying things like, 'Look out for the Hun in the sun' and 'I see old Babsworth bought it.' Then before you could say 'Jolly good show' somebody yelled 'scramble' and in no time at all they'd be swooping on the ME109s which fell from the sky in a trail of smoke as our cheers shook the cinema. The only naval epic I remember was (I think) *In Which We Serve*. It starred Noel Coward and I seem to remember how relieved we all were that he sunk before he had a chance to sing.

After six years of the real thing, audiences were more than ready for a change of pace, and that's what they got as our screens filled with a cavalcade of comedies. England spawned a host of 'funny men' who seemed to churn out a movie a week although many of them didn't look as if they'd taken that long to put together. Tommy Trinder wore a funny hat and smiled a lot and said 'You lucky people'. Arthur Askey wore a funny hat and smiled a lot and still sang about bumblebees. Old Mother Riley wore a funny hat and a shawl. I'm not sure if Franky Randell wore a hat or not because he was more famous for not wearing his false teeth and saying 'Get of me foot' while a cockney called Syd Fields made England's first (and the world's worst) musical which was so bad we could hardly sit through it twice.

Once in a while these comedic classics gave way to a string of dramas which we generally considered to be soft as clarts but which our parents couldn't get enough of. Black-hearted villains (always played by James Mason) pursued sweet young maidens with heaving bosoms (always played by Patricia Roc) while sensitive young men (played by either Stewart Granger or Lawrence Olivier) tried to save her and at the same time stay out of the clutches of the evil temptress with an even heavier heaving, and lower cut, bosom (always played by Margaret Lockwood). These epics were always set in great gloomy mansions where candles flickered mysteriously, waves crashed at the bottom of rugged cliffs, mists hung permanently over harsh desolate moors and fearsome gales smashed windows open in a swirl of velvet curtains just as our hero was coming to the end of a proper concerto on the grand piano.

Our appetite for adventure and high drama wasn't catered for solely by British studios. Geordie kids in scuffed shoes and hand me down clothes, swaggered the streets, rat-tat-tatting make believe tommy guns and snarling 'You dirty rat' or 'OK Fatso this is for Lefty and Big Al' depending on whether they'd seen James Cagney or Edward G. Robinson the night before. You could almost smell the cordite wafting out of the cinema door as Scarface or Dillinger and their assorted mobs held up banks, bootlegged, and spent more time on the running boards of their old cars than they ever did in the flash interiors. These classic gangster movies always had a sad ending as far as we kids were concerned because American film regulations demanded that good must always prevail over evil so, inevitably, the bloke we were cheering for either tramped off defiantly to his cell in the big house or even worse slumped slowly to the floor as the fifty-first FBI bullet finally brought him undone.

No such fate was in store, however, for our number one all-American hero – Tarzan! We never realised till many years later that Tarzan was in fact a very British creation but by then he was so firmly fixed in our hearts and minds in the shape of Johnny Weisemuller that it's extremely doubtful we'd have been anywhere near as enthusiastic if Arthur Askey had played the part. Our blood chilled and pulses raced as our hero criss-crossed darkest Africa, swinging from tree to tree on his way to wrestle the Indian tiger or dive into the pool where that forty foot Amazonian crocodile always awaited him. It was a sign of those unsexy times that he had his arms around that croc far more than he ever did around Jane in her designer mini skirt. And we loved Cheetah the chimp that turned somersaults and stuck its lip out and chattered and chimped as it led Tarzan unerringly to where Boy was just about to be sacrificed by the Umgabi pygmies. This must have created terrible problems for the scriptwriters who had to find more words for Cheetah than they did for the star but they managed OK.

As we sat cackling over the comedies or gunning with the gangsters, there was only one thing that any of us wanted more than a Tarzan movie and that was our sixteenth birthday! By today's standards, there was little to get over exited about in an age when screen kisses were timed with a stopwatch and even Ma and Pa Kettle didn't go to bed together. Despite this, films were still classified and naturally enough, the ones we'd give our back teeth to see were restricted to elderly seventeen-year-olds or those accompanied by an adult. The Comedy theatre seemed to get most of the 'H' for Horror movies that we longed to see. Determined to defeat this blatant discrimination, we'd saunter up the alley, top coat collars turned up and fag end drooping nonchalantly from our lip a la Humphrey Bogart style, to the pay box where we'd ask for 'One adult please' in a voice that was supposed to be a manly baritone but which was more like a boy soprano with laryngitis. Peering sceptically through her tiny window, the little old lady would ask in a resigned sort of way how old we were, to which we'd reply 'sixteen' in a voice that was intended to convey both shock and surprise that she'd ask such a stupid question. In the next part of this well rehearsed charade, she'd pick on the shortest of our stunted bunch and enquire exactly when he'd attained this grand old age to which he'd confess that it had in fact been just the week before. If business was even worse than usual, she'd shake her head and tut a few times before tearing off the tickets but most times she'd dispatch us with barely a second glance as we retreated snarling threats never to darken her rotten doors again even when we were legally old enough to do so. Which might still have been anything up to two years hence.

The first time she let me past her mini-fortress was to see a Frankenstein movie that all the older kids had been raving on about and after about twenty minutes I was wishing she'd knocked me back. Thunder rumbled, lightning flashed and I just knew that the huge monster with the bolt in its neck was going to lurch to its feet if that daft bugger in the cape didn't stop twiddling with those knobs. Emerging later all pallid and soaked in an icy cold sweat, we'd laugh among ourselves about how we knew it wasn't a real monster and how we'd felt like laughing out loud when it smashed through the door and how we couldn't understand why you had to be sixteen to watch rubbish like that. Then we went home and had nightmares for a fortnight.

The 'lying about your age technique' was only adopted in extreme circumstances, particularly, if like myself, you suffered from stunted growth and a face that refused to age until much later in life when it galloped off at a million miles an hour. Far more reliable was the generally adopted routine that saw us scrubbed and wearing our best jumper and a meekly grovelling expression as we asked every adult with a kind face, 'Would you take us in please?' Nobody saw anything unusual in having to run the gauntlet of pleading kids each clutching his half-price ticket money and each putting on performances that would have brought tears to the eyes of a hardened Delhi beggar. Invariably, a man or woman or couple would give you the nod, pay for you at the ticket window then take you inside where both parties went their own way. One of the proudest days of my life occurred long after I'd passed the age of assent, when the first time a young kid sidled up to me and asked if I'd take him in. Not only did I take him in, I almost paid for him out of my own limited resources to celebrate his recognition of my manhood. Almost.

While all of this was going on outside the cinema, great changes were taking place on the inside. Colour was rapidly replacing the familiar black and white. Now Robin stood resplendent in his dashing green pantyhose, the previously black and white Red Indians showed up in a coppery tone that was close enough to what we'd imagined but the natives who said stuff like 'Umgabi Bwana' to 'Sanders Of The River' weren't all that much different. Soon our postage stamp screens would expand and bend and stretch until they almost reached from one side of the theatre to the other except, of course, at The Howard where they were still debating whether sound was just another passing fad.

My wife Ethel and I went all the way to Whitley Bay (a full fifteen minutes and fourpence each on the bus) to see *Quo Vadis* our very first Cinemascope epic and, the then, ultimate cinematic experience. Chariots charged from left to right, lions chased hymn singing Christians in the opposite direction, swords clashed, crosses burned and colourful Roman soldiers in brightly Brasso'd armour delivered memorable lines like, 'Hey Centoorian, what noos from Joolius?' We'd only just started to adapt to all this gee whizzery when one of the big cinemas in the Newcastle Haymarket announced the arrival of 3D. After standing in an even longer than usual queue of like-minded thrill-seekers, we finally arrived at the ticket window where, in return for our two bob, we got not only the usual ticket but a pair of cardboard framed glasses as well. As the starting time of the main feature approached, the screen instructed us to don our spectacles and gave appropriate warnings to those cretins who tried to read the *Evening Chronicle* through them. Then, like a bunch of absolute Wallies, we sat there with one green and one red eye watching cowboys jump out of the screen while Indians fired flaming arrows into the upper circle and all the young girls clung on to their partner's arms and screamed dutifully. It required a considerable degree of concentration to balance the glasses far enough up your nose to obtain the desired three-dimensional effect but this was no bad thing as it tended to keep your mind off the fact that the movie itself was a terrible load of old cobblers.

The same couldn't be said of the continuous stream of musicals that enthralled us through the late 1940s and '50s. Every week seemed to herald a new offering, each more colourful and tuneful than the one we'd raved over the week before. Queues grew longer than ever as we marvelled at the tapping of Fred Astaire's twinkling toes, the ballet like gyrations of Gene Kelly and the comedic cavorting of Donald O'Connor. And what about their glistening, glamorous partners who sang and swirled and swayed their way from the romantic left bank of Paris to the soaking streets of downtown Manhattan. Ginger Rogers, Leslie Caron, Betty Grable, Anne Miller, Mitzi Gaynor, Doris Day and Vera Ellen who I fell so madly in love with that I even invested in an airmail request for an autographed photograph which, as of this week, still hasn't arrived. Tenors bellowed their lungs out as we held heated debates over whether Mario Lanza was better than Howard Keel or whether Deanna Durbin could out-soprano Kathryn Grayson. And what about the musicals themselves? Slaves toted bales of cotton and hummed and swayed as the Showboat meandered up the mighty Mississippi, Annie got Her Gun, Gordon McCrea went to the great Carousel in the sky while a fat lady sang *You'll Never Walk Alone* and there wasn't a soccer hooligan in sight. Judy went Over The Rainbow, Gene danced on bin lids while he Sang In The Rain, Calamity Jane (looking and sounding awfully like Doris Day) galloped off into the Black Hills Of Dakota where she went on about her Secret Love while Bing pledged his True Love to the delectable Princess Grace. There were Blue Skies and White Christmas, Three Little Words and Seven Brides For Seven Brothers, Americans in Paris and Frenchmen in the South Pacific who weren't setting off atom bombs. Then followed a spate of musical biographies as Tyrone Power learned to play the piano for the Eddie Duchin Story, James Stewart blew a trumpet just like Glen Miller and Larry Parkes blackened his face and mimed his way through the two Jolson pictures that I sat through more times than the projectionist.

None of us who lived through those glorious years could have guessed that within a couple of decades, the queues would melt away, the screens would shrink and revert to black and white and move into our living rooms or that finally most of these hallowed halls would suffer the ultimate indignity of becoming Bingo Parlours. Audiences that once sat breathlessly waiting the unguessed at denouement of the latest Hitchcock movie, now sat just as breathlessly awaiting all the twos twenty two or on its own, blind five. Where Carmen Miranda once shook her maracas, previously respectable old ladies like my Mum exhorted the caller to shake his balls and the Sound Of Music became the sound of mucus as the deathly silence was broken only by the call of the numbers and the shushes of the half deaf as Woodbine smokers tried desperately to muffle their death rattles.

And finally there was them mighty lads. As someone who has watched most sports at just about every level from local to international, nothing has ever come close to those Saturday afternoons at St James' Park. The good natured cheers as the little old bloke leading the Coxlodge Institute Brass Band dropped his mace and almost got trampled to death by his deeply concentrating bandsmen as he bent to pick it up. The shouts as youngsters were tossed and tumbled as they were passed hand over hand over the heads of the densely packed crowd. The sense of spine tingling anticipation as the band departed and the spontaneous roar from sixty thousand Geordie throats as the first black and white shirt emerged from the tunnel. The pregnant silence as the opposition emerged, the increasing tension as the captains tossed and apprehension as both teams sorted themselves out for the kick-off. Then, as the action got underway, the cheers, the 'oohs' and 'aahs' and heartfelt moans and then that great soaring swelling roar that told folks miles away that Wor Jackie or one of them other heroes had smashed one in for the lads. Jammed into the densely packed crowd, we swayed up and down the open terraces sweating under our greatcoats despite the freezing grey afternoon. The icy feeling as the other mob hit the crossbar with our goalie beaten and the warm glow around your ankles as someone behind got rid of a couple of pints of recycled Newcastle Brown Ale. The sheer joy of sitting in the bus afterwards reliving the winning goal that would be discussed analysed and dissected over the remainder of the weekend and well into the working week.

There were also those rare days when we headed home valiant and unlucky losers, but losers nevertheless. Beaten by an offside goal three minutes after the ref should have blown full time if his cheap watch hadn't stopped. Then we'd sit wrapped in the sort of sombre silence you get when people gather to watch a royal funeral. Conversations were muted and kids who dared giggle or make too much noise got a clip around the ear for their lack of sensitivity and even the conductor looked embarrassed when he was forced to intrude on our grief for such a mundane item as a return ticket. But time heals all wounds and after ten or twelve days the pain would ease enough for us to start thinking about the next game because it was our only pleasure.

And that is what we did before TV – basically nothing worth writing home about.

SECTION EIGHT

LOOKING BACK

Norman Christenson.

Looking back on all of this, it's hard to imagine that it's sixty odd years since those Gypsies left me on the door step of those poor (but honest folk) in Victoria Street.

It certainly wouldn't be appropriate for me to speculate on how I've turned out after all that life has heaped on these puny shoulders, but it is interesting to look at some of the predictions made on my behalf. The long blonde hair that hung over my eyes, didn't send me cock-eyed as Grandma Mac always swore it would, although this could be attributed to the fact that it is some considerable time that hair of any description hung anywhere near my eyes.

Wor Ma was obviously wrong when she repeatedly forecast that I'd still be sat under her feet reading a book when I was fifty and the headmaster who saw me 'doing well at carpentry and joinery' was no nearer the mark. The person who did go closest to getting it right was none other than Professor Omar, a man whose fearless forecasts were world famous all over Whitley Bay. Sat in his caravan in the summer of 1955, he predicted that I would marry someone who had something to do with wool, I'd travel far, have two kids and live in a wide fronted house with lawns in front. Ethel, my wife-to-be, did work at the Great Northern Knitwear, Australia is certainly about as far as you can get

Norman with sister Doreen and Wor Ma on her last visit to Australia in 1990. She suffered a massive heart attack and died just a few weeks after she returned to Shields. She was a far better Ma than any of us deserved.

The Australian branch of the Christensons. Left to right: son Paul, his wife Virginia, Norman, Ethel and daughter Linda.

from Whitley Bay, I did end up with two kids and my house is white fronted and sits behind lawns that are as impressive as any in the street.

I've travelled to every State in Australia plus New Zealand and Japan and Taiwan and Fiji and Europe and even the good old US of A. I climbed the corporate ladder, shared the executive toilet and even rated a minute entry in *The Who's Who of Australian Business*. In later years, I achieved some small fame as a regular contributor to the letters page of the *Sydney Morning Herald* and even had my two minutes of fame when a television current affairs programme included me in their coverage of eminent letter writers. And in the process, I've met so many wonderful people and had so much fun.

Everybody loves their kids but I've been blessed with two I really like. The quiet Paul who always calls me Norm and who smiles and shakes his head at me and the not so quiet Linda who is still with us although she nearly died one year when she reckoned it was only a game after Newcastle had lost yet another Cup Final.

And then there's Ethel who makes the best sandwiches in the world and who, after almost half a century, is undoubtedly the best thing that ever happened to me. In more recent years, our family has been extended to include daughter in law Virginia and the two most

Norman's grand-daughters, Isabella (almost three) and Alana (just turned one).

beautiful grand-daughters in the entire world as the photograph quite clearly shows.

Of course it would be foolish to claim that life has been just one long laugh. I do, occasionally, get depressed when I realise that I'm probably my richest relative and it would be nice to beat the golf course just a few more times than it beats me. But life wasn't meant to be easy and, as they used to say to Derek on his regular trips to the infirmary, a little bit of pain never hurt anyone.

Thanks to everyone who helped get this labour of love on to paper. Hopefully, it may have revived other memories of a canny old town and the canny people who inhabited it. I'd love to hear from anyone who may have enjoyed any of this but please keep it to yourself if you haven't.

Ta Ra.

Norman Christenson

Acknowledgements

The author and publishers would like to thank the following who have assisted in the production:

Julia Stafford and the staff of North Tyneside Library, without whose support this book would never seen the light of day. Editor Andrew Clark, who somehow pulled it together despite having to work with someone he'd never met on the other side of the world. Harry Clark who was a great help with his internet expertise. Eric Hollerton, George Nairn, Kevin Brady and cousin Alan McDonald who provided most of the photographs and last but by no means least my wife Ethel who read every word and reckoned every one was brilliant.

Cooksons Athletic AFC, 1927-28. The team were Northern Amateur League Second Division Champions, League Charity Cup Winners and Tynemouth Dispensary Cup Winners. Two of Norman Christenson's uncles were in the side – John and Tom.

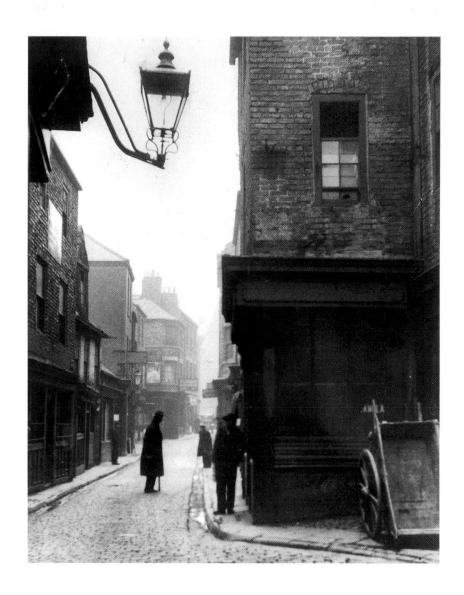

The People's History

To find out more about this unique series of local history books – and to receive a catalogue of the latest titles – send a large stamped addressed envelope to:

The People's History Ltd
Suite 1
Byron House
Seaham Grange Business Park
Seaham
County Durham
SR7 0PY